Ahsan Academy of Research
(Springs, South Africa)

Encounter between Faith and Materialism: An Analytical Study of Surah Al-Kahf

Sayyid Abul Hasan Ali Nadwi

Edited by
Abdul Kader Choughley

Tawasul International
Centre for Publishing, Research and Dialogue

First Edition 2021
ISBN 978-93-90167-81-4

Edited by Abdul Kader Choughley

Translated by Abdur Raheem Kidwai
Ahsan Academy of Research
(Springs, South Africa)
info@ahsanacademy.co.za
www.ahsanacademy.co.za

Tawasul International
Centre for Publishing, Research and Dialogue, Rome, Italy

CONTENTS

Preface

The present book owes its origin to my book in Arabic, *Al-Sirā' bayn al-Imān wa al-Māddiyah* published in 1971 by Dar Al-Qalam, Kuwait.

The contents of the book explain how it came into existence and the stages of its evolution, its sources and their analysis, its relevance to our times and the guidance provided by Surah Al-Kahf.

It is hoped that its study will help fathom the truths embodied in this Surah, in particular, and the Qur'an in general.

All help and support is from Allah alone.

23 Muharram 1392   Abul Hasan Ali Nadwi 10

March 1972   Rae Bareli, India

INTRODUCTION

How I studied Surah Al-Kahf first

From my early childhood it has been my routine to recite certain Qur'anic Surahs on every Friday. Among these is Surah Al-Kahf.[1] The *ahādith* exhort that Surah Al-Kahf be recited and memorized. It is prescribed as the protection against *Dajjāl*.[2]

On studying these *ahādith* I decided to study closely this Surah in order to identify its levels of meaning, truths, warnings and strategies which may defend one against *Dajjāl*. The Prophet (peace be upon him) often sought protection against *Dajjāl* and has urged the Muslim community to seek refuge against it. For it will be the last, final mischief and trial. The Prophet (peace be upon him) is on record saying: "Since the birth of Adam until the Last Day the most important event is the emergence of *Dajjāl*." I reflected as to why the Prophet (peace be upon him), who was most familiar with

---

[1] I owe this routine to the upbringing of my esteemed mother. She always exhorted me to recite Surah Al-Kahf on every Friday. Often did she ask me whether I was doing so or not. As I recited this Surah many times, I memorized it. My mother (new the entire Qur'an by heart and stood out for her study of writings on Islam. She was gifted with poetic abilities. Her supplications to Allah and poems in the praise of Prophet Muhammad (peace be upon him) are reflective of her conviction and innermost feelings. Her poetical works have literary merits as well. She passed away in Jumadi al-Awwal 1388H.

[2] Abu Sa'id Khudri reports: "One who reads Surah Al- Kahf as it was recited will be safe against *Dajjāl*, if it appears in his day. *Dajjāl* will not find a way to gain any control over him." (*Mustadrak* by Hakim). In *Mukhtarah* Ibn Mardawiyah has recounted on Ali's authority that the Prophet (peace be upon him) said: "He who recites Surah Al-Kahf on Fridays will be safe against mischief for the whole week. If *Dajjāl* appears in his day, he will be safe against his mischief as well." Abu Al-Darda reports the Prophet (peace be upon him) saying: "He who recites the first ten verses of Surah Al-Kahf (or its last ten verses, according to a variant report) will be immune against *Dajjāl's* mischief." (Muslim, Abu Dawud, Tirmidhi. Tirmidhi speaks of the last three verses in this context). It is recorded in *Musnad Ahmad*: "He who recites the last ten verses of Surah Al-Kahf will be protected against *Dajjāl's* mischief." (6: 446-449). Nasai records this report: "He who recites ten verses of Surah Al-Kahf, this will serve as his protection and security against *Dajjāl*." Several *ahādith* of the same import are on record. *Sahih Muslim* (Narrated by 'Imran ibn Husayn).

the Qur'an and its deeper meaning, singled out this particular Surah.

Relevance of this Surah to the turmoil of our era

I felt strongly that I should unravel this secret. I was seen on discovering the excellence of this Surah and how it helps defend against the mischief, of which the Prophet (peace be upon him) has given the tiding.

The Qur'an consists of many Surahs, both long and short ones. Why was this particular Surah selected? Why does it have this special feature?[3]

I knew that it is a unique Surah which provides protection against all mischiefs, of which the biggest one is represented by *Dajjāl*. It stands out as the antidote to the toxic effects of *Dajjāl* and can cure its victims, provided that one assimilates the meaning and message of this Surah. And this can be achieved by memorizing it and reciting it frequently. One who does so will be protected against this terrible mischief and will not fall a prey to its machinations.

Contained in this Surah are such guiding principles, clear indications, parables and illustrations which may help in identifying *Dajjāl* at any place and in any era. It can alert one to the basis of this mischief on which it rests. Moreover, the study of this Surah inspirits one's heart and mind with a view to taking on *Dajjāl* and to rise in revolt against it. It is characterized by a spirit which categorically and forcefully refutes *Jāhilliyyah* and its votaries, and their way of life. It strives a fatal blow against their mindset.

---

[3] This stance is shared by many eminent scholars, especially of *tafsir* and *hadith*. They have arrived at the conclusion that this Surah is closely linked with the mischief posed by *Dajjāl*. 'Allamah Muhammad Tāhir Patani (d. 986H) has cited some classical authorities in his *Majma' Bahār al-Anwār* to this effect: "The excellence of this Surah is in relation to the mischief created by *Dajjāl*. He would appear in the later times. The protection may be similar to that of the people of the Cave against that tyrannical king or against every deceiver who resorts to fraud. The Surah abounds in wonderful signs. One who recites it will not be vulnerable to any mischief. In my opinion, Prophet Muhammad (peace be upon him) was aware of the special feature of this Surah." (*Majma' Bahār al-Anwār*, entry: "Dajjāl").

Unity of theme in this Surah

With these ideas in mind, I turned to the Surah for studying it afresh. My notions served as a light for exploring its meaning and message. As I embarked upon its study, I realized that it stands out as a universe of new ideas, with which I had been so far unfamiliar. I discovered that it represents a single theme which I can describe as the encounter between Faith and Materialism or a conflict between the unseen power and material resources. All the parables, allusions, sermons and analogies in this Surah bear out the same theme, explicitly as well as implicitly.

I felt elated over this discovery. This was a new facet of Prophet Muhammad's Prophethood and of the miracles of the Qur'an, which captivated me. I had no idea that the book revealed in the seventh century, some thirteen hundred years ago, contains such a graphic picture of the culture and civilization conceived and developed by *Dajjāl,* which was born is seventeenth century and has matured in twentieth century. The Prophet (peace be upon him) spoke of the same as *Dajjāl,* of which we now see the culmination.

Twenty-five years ago when I was the teacher of *tafsir* at Dar al-'Ulum, Nadwah (India), I wrote these articles which were published in *Tarjumān al-Qur'ān* edited by Sayyid Abul A'la Mawdudi. During the same period I stayed for a few days with Mawlana Sayyid Manazir Ahsan Gilani, Chairman, Department of Theology, Osmania University, Hyderabad. It was in 1946. Every night I discussed some scholarly issues with him. He told me that he had read my articles and informed me that he was engaged in writing an extensive article on the same topic, which will be published in *al-Furqān* (published by Mawlana Muhammad Manzur Nu'mani). After his death when the issue of *al-Furqān* came out, it carried the same article.

The publication of his article prompted me to study again Surah Al-Kahf and to publish my observations on it. I intended to bring out the relevance of this Surah to the later day mischiefs, movements, mission, philosophies and thought patterns. It was also aimed at drawing attention to the lessons and clues embedded in this Surah. So I jotted down all that came to my mind by Allah's leave. Though I was not a formal student of Mawlana Gilani, I regarded him as my teacher. He was gracious enough to treat me as a dear brother. I drew on some of the points, hints and the Qur'an interpretation contained in his article. My analysis of this Surah is not on the traditional pattern which is usually followed by *mufassirun*. Rather, it is the outpouring of my innermost thoughts and a general thematic overview of Surah Al-Kahf.

How to understand *Dajjal*

The very title *Dajjāl*[4] represents the key to decoding its personality and to measure its depths and what distinguishes it from all other votaries of evil, corruption, unbelief and atheism. It is notorious by this title and all of its activities reflect its traits.

The malaise of the present materialistic civilization is its pretence and deception.[5] It has impacted everything. For the labels which are used conceal the contents. There is a general and popular trend for terminology and jargon. However, there is no intrinsic link between the outward appearance and its inner quality. There is no correspondence between the beginning and conclusion, and theory and practice. Same holds true for the buzzwords and slogans which have been substituted for religion. These have cast a spell on man's mind and heart. The statements of ideologues are sanctified and their adulation is encouraged. Any doubt about their integrity is construed as conservatism and negation of something evident. Even the sharpest and best minds have been deceived on this count,

---

[4] In his *Lisān al-'Arab* Ibn Manzur states: "*Al-Dajjāl* stands for a deceiver and liar. *Dajjāl* is its derivative. *Dajjāl* is designated also as the false *Masih*. For he would resort to magic and lies. According to Ibn Khalawiyah, Abu Amr has explained well *Dajjāl*. For him, *Dajjāl* signifies a fraudster or pretender. According to Al-Azhari, every liar is a *Dajjāl*. For he says one thing but does another. In the opinion of Abu Al-'Abbas, he is known as *Dajjāl* because he will deceive people and present evil in a pleasing manner." (*Lisān al-'Arab*. Abridged).

[5] Hudhaifah ibn Al-Yaman states: "*Dajjāl* will appear, accompanied with fire and water. What people will take as water will actually be corroding fire. Likewise, what would appear as fire will in reality be sweet water." (Muslim, "Kitab al-Fitan wa Ashrat al-Sa'ah"). Abu Hurayrah reports: "He will carry something like Paradise and Hell. What he will project as Paradise will actually be Hell."

though they are exceptionally gifted persons in their own right. For they have fallen a prey to false philosophies and movements and endorse them unquestioningly. Without ascertaining the sincerity and truthfulness of the votaries of these movements they are seen supporting them warmly. They lack moral courage to adjudge their success or failure. They do not assess their loss or benefit to humanity and still stand for them. They are not ready to check whether these movements lead to any real, abiding success and ensure natural rights to mankind or not. They are carried away by their deception and the greater *Dajjāl* moves on with its followers who are equally deceptive. This holds true for all phases of history.

This *Dajjāl* mindest has permeated the present civilization so deeply that it opposes such seminal and sacred doctrines as Prophethood, the Hereafter, the Unseen, the Creator of the universe, the faith in Allah's perfect power, shari'ah and teachings. It relies only on the outward appearance and focuses on such items or paraphernalia which may gratify man's bodily desires, immediate gains and apparent success. All these incidents and parables and their resultant lessons are linked with this central theme and constitute an interlinking thread.

Construction of culture and civilization and providing guidance to mankind: Identical roles of Judaism and Christianity

We have to state this truth regretfully that Christianity which led Europe in the Dark Ages and the rebellious Judaism played an identical role, notwithstanding basic differences in their creed. Both of them contributed to diverting the whole human civilization to gross materialism which is wholly devoid of the teachings of Prophets and spiritualism. Both of them are responsible, in an equal degree, for the plight of mankind.

The Christian nations had freed themselves from the yoke of Church and Pope and their ties with true Christianity which is peace loving and stands for pure monotheism, had weakened, if not severed. They switched over to the fast paced, extremist materialistic path. Eventually, as a result of the latest discoveries and invention of devastating items the whole humanity is pitted against a horrible danger. The requisite balance between knowledge and passions, reason and conscience and nature and morals has vanished.

Perhaps for these reasons this Surah has a close connection with Christianity and Judaism. Rather, the Surah opens with a reference to the Christian dogma:

> All praise belongs to Allah Who sent the Book to His servant. There is no defect in it. It is straight and clear. It warns against Allah's terrible punishment. It gives good news to the believers who do good that there is excellent reward for them. They will live in Paradise forever. It warns those who say that Allah has taken to Himself a son. Neither they nor their forefathers had any knowledge about it. It is something monstrous that comes from their mouths. What they say is totally a lie.

(18: 1-5)

The Western civilization which has developed under the shadow of Christianity, rather under its patronage, is too much devoted to this ephemeral life. The desire to prolong life and make it as comfortable as possible is deep rooted. Furthermore, it negates moral values, and relies much on material resources and total engagement with worldliness. At this focal point Judaism, notwithstanding its opposition to and rivalry with Christianity, has joined hands with it.

In this Surah Allah has condemned polytheism (*shirk*) and the doctrine of the Sonship which is peculiar to Christianity. Likewise, it censures worship of this worldly life, deeming it to be permanent, and being engrossed in it while severing relations with all else. The Qur'an underscores the limited nature of the world:

> Allah has made everything on earth pleasing in order to test as to who does good actions. (In the end) He will make the earth a plain field.

(18: 7-8)

While rebuking those given to worldliness, rejecting the

Hereafter and being negligent, the Qur'an proclaims:

> Say: "Should I tell you of those whose actions lead to their loss? Those whose all efforts are wasted for the life of this world. They, however, imagine that they are doing something good."

(18: 103-104)

The doctrine of the Hereafter, and belief in the Unseen and the Creator of the universe and His perfect power permeate the entire Surah. This belief system, psyche, rational outlook and temperament is at odds, with the materialistic mindset and psychology. Materialism relies only on sense perception, observation and experiment. It celebrates worldly gains, pleasures of the flesh and nationalistic and ethnic superiority. The religious outlook loathes all this. Rather, with all the force at its command, religion takes it head-on. This Surah carries an antidote to that materialism which, as part of divine dispensation, has gripped mostly Christians. Throughout history they have been its patron and custodian. Among them the 'Great' *Dajjāl* will appear who will be the biggest champion of unbelief, atheism, fraud and deception.

Prophet Muhammad (peace be upon him) is on record having observed: "This Surah, particularly the recitation of its early part protects one against mischief."

Thus there is a subtle line between the beginning and end of the Surah which every reader can experience. Overall, its nexus with *Dajjāl* is very strong, a point which we will elaborate later.

Four stories in this Surah

This Surah comprises four stories which serve as its cornerstones. In other words, these are the axis around which its teachings, lessons, admonition and wisdom revolve:

- Story of the People of the Cave
- Story of the Owner of the two Gardens
- Story of the Prophet Musa (peace be upon him) and Khidr (peace be upon him)
- Story of Dhū l-Qarnayn

In terms of their style and context these stories are distinct from one another. However, their spirit and underlying message are identical. So thematically these are interconnected, representing a well-knit whole.

Two worldviews

Our universe is subject, in usual circumstances, to natural laws and causes which have been at work. These forces of nature dominate the working of the universe. Only in exceptional cases these laws of nature cease to function. So those who focus only on the natural law of cause and effect, and are restricted to this material and tangible world believe that cause and effect is the only law at work in our world. For them certain causes bring about certain results and there is no force in the universe which may impede or reverse this phenomenon. It is inconceivable for them that a power may change altogether this arrangement at His will and may create something even without any natural cause. So this group has a narrow outlook regarding external factors. They have even deified these natural laws. They acknowledge natural properties of things and resources. However, they reject the existence of any power who may be deemed as the only Master and Ruler of this universe, without any partner and whose decree prevails in the universe. They deny also Life after Death, the grand assembly and divine recompense. On the contrary, they have devoted fully their energy and talents to tapping and mastering the natural forces, to identifying properties of things and to amassing material resources. This has been their own goal. Owing to such devotion they have developed deep love and regard for material objects. Rather, they take these to be their Lord and objects of worship. They deny every force other than these. They are obsessed with achieving their goals. Once they made things subservient to them, they claimed divinity, implicitly or explicitly. For example, they enslaved fellow human beings and played havoc with others' lives, belongings and honour. For glorifying their nation, motherland or ideological party they perpetrated all sorts of excesses on their victims.

The other worldview is distinctly different from the above one, in its belief system and strategy. This worldview is premised on the conviction there is a Supreme Power beyond and above the natural causes, forces of nature, material goods and their properties. That Mighty Power controls and governs all of these. Their working is dependent upon Allah's will. All causes and effect are because of only His command. As Allah intends, He brings into being everything. He manages things and divests these of the law of causation when He wills. For every cause and effect is under His total control. He is the prime cause and mover.

The cause and effect chain concludes with Him. He never abandoned this universe even for a moment after having created it. The law of causation is subservient to Him. Nothing can disobey or rebel against Him. No one in the heavens or on earth can defeat His plan. Out of His perfect wisdom and absolute power, He has invested things with their properties and causes with effect. He conjoins and severs, and creates and destroys things. It is He Who brings into existence everything out of nothing and produces all beings:

Whenever He wills a thing, He only says: "Be", and it is.

(36:82)

The above verse asserts that certain factors are at work in the universe which have a greater bearing on the fate of individuals and communities than the physical and material forces. Likewise, their effects are also more substantial than the ones accruing from the chain and effect cause.

These factors are: faith, good deeds, excellent morals and manners, obedience to and worship of Allah, justice and fairness, love and kindness and other virtues and values. Going by the same analogy, factors such as unbelief and rebellion, corruption on earth, wrongdoing and gratifying the self and sins and evil deeds have negative impact.

If one leads a life full of values, without abandoning physical factors, the universe will work in tandem with him and he will enjoy a peaceful and meaningful life. Allah will facilitate things for him. At time, laws of nature will be made to work in his favour and supernatural effects may appear. In contrast, he who is engrossed in evil factors while relying on physical forces alone and constructs his life on that basis alone, the forces of nature will turn hostile to him.

The very forces tapped by him will stab him in the back and he will become dependent upon these. Nature will be pitted against him and natural forces will obstruct his movement.

The encounter between Faith and Materialism in this Surah

Surah Al-Kahf presents an account of the clash between two doctrines, two ideologies and two mindsets. One of these stands for materialism and reliance on material factors whereas the other one signifies faith in the unseen and in Allah. It spells out the belief system, deeds, morals and consequences contingent upon both the viewpoints. It warns against materialism and reliance on it while rejecting Allah and the unseen forces.

Chapter 1

STORY OF THE PEOPLE OF THE CAVE

Let us turn our attention to the four stories related in this Surah. The first one is the story of the People of the Cave and the Inscription. Who were they? What is the worth and relevance of this story in history? Why has the Qur'an immortalized this account which will be recounted again and again?

People of the Cave in the Christian and Religious tradition

Before we take up this story in the Qur'an in its inimitable style, purposive and graceful presentation and rhetorical features, we will identify its antecedents in the ancient Scriptures and popular tradition. It is worth clarifying that the Qur'anic account is free from all unnecessary details. This story has also been part of the oral tradition, transmitted by generations upon generations. Later, we will examine the common points and divergence between their and Qur'anic accounts.

The story of the People of the Cave does not feature in the Old Testament. For this incident had happened in the early days of Christianity, as its message of monotheism (*tawhid*) and abandoning idolatry had been spread by the Christian apostles. By then the books of the Old Testament had been compiled. This story highlights the heroic achievement and consistency of the belief of the followers of Prophet 'Isa (peace be upon him) and hence it had no appeal for the Jews to record it. In contrast, it was the most popular story among Christians. What accounts for it is that in comparison to other stories, it is full of fascinating events. Moreover, it underscores the resolve, conviction, and self sacrifice of the early Christians in the cause of their faith. It throws light also on their religious fervour for the sake of the early pure teachings of Christianity. This account revives even today one's latent faith, fervour and commitment against falsehood. These aspects of this story have given it a permanent place in history and made it so popular in a vast area of the earth. It has been transmitted from one era to another and by one generation to another. Let us ascertain how it was understood by the earlier Christians and their comments on it for future generations.

Below is the summary of the article on it in the *Enclyclopaedia of Religion and Ethics*.[1]

The story of the Seven Sleepers is a story of some holy persons, which is rational and convincing, and highly popular in the world. Its outline, as appearing in the ancient sources, is as follows: "The emperor Decius sought to revive idolatry in the town of Ephesus.[2] He asked the locals, especially Christians to make offerings at idols. As a result, the Christians abandoned Christianity. However, one group among them adhered to their faith and put up with state persecution. In the same period seven youths (some reports put their number at eight), who had been staying in the royal palace appeared before the emperor.

The emperor charged them with having secretly accepted Christianity. There is divergence in reports about their names. These youths refused to present any offering at the altar. The emperor granted them a month-long respite for mending their ways, giving up Christianity and after this decree the emperor left that town.

The youths too, left the town and hid in a cave in the Anchilus

---

[1] The celebrated British historian, Gibbon has discussed this story in his *Decline and Fall of the Roman Empire*. His critique betrays his partisanship for Christianity and his uncalled for, uncharitable comments on Islam. See vol. 2: 241-243. Modern Library Giant Series, USA.

[2] Most of *tafsir* writers such as Baydhawi, Nishapuri, Alusi and Ibn Kathir have opined that it was the town of Ephesus. This view is shared also by most of the historians and geographers. Gibbon too, endorses this view. (See his section, "Seven Sleepers"). As to its geographical location, it is reported in Bustani's *Encyclopaedia* that it is one of the towns in Anatolia, to the south of Qaistrah canal, sixty kilometres away from Izmir. The Romans had made it the capital of their Western Asia province. It was a flourishing trade centre. Its main attraction, nonetheless, was the grand temple of the Greek god, Diana, which is one of the seven wonders of the word and houses the biggest Greek idol. In his book, *A Manual of Bible History*, Blackie reports that in ancient times Ephesus was notorious for the debauchery of its people. It was the den of degeneration and perversion. Both the Eastern and Western forms of idolatry were practised there.

mountain. One of them, Diomedes, who had changed his name to Lambuchus, returned to town, disguised as a poor person, in order to collect news and to secure food supply. After a few days the emperor returned to the town and ordered that those youths be produced before him. Diomedes informs his friends of the royal order.

They take food and are worried over the order. It is then that Allah imposes upon them a long, deep sleep. When the youths do not report, their parents are summoned. They plead that they had no hand in their escape and inform him of their hiding in the cave in the Anchilus mountain. At the emperor's command, that cave is sealed so that those youths die inside it and lie buried there. Two Christians, Theodore and Rufinus, write their account on a brass sheet and this Inscription is installed at the mouth of the cave.

After 307 years a rebellion broke out during the reign of the emperor Theodosius II, led by some Christians. A Christian group headed by Theodore rejects the doctrines of the Life after Death and the resurrection of the body which disturbs the Christian emperor. Meanwhile, Allah impels a local chief, Adolious to erect a fence beside the same cave. As masons take out some stones, the mouth of the cave opens. Allah wakes up those youths. They think that they had slept only for one night. They once again discuss the issue of their belief and resolve to lay down their lives, rather than follow the Emperor Decius's command. Diomedes goes to town and is amazed to note the symbol of the cross at the town gate. He asks a passer-by whether it is the same town of Ephesus. He is eager to inform his friends of this transformation. However, he first buys food and pays some coins of Decius's time. The shopkeeper thinks that the youth had laid his hands on a treasure trove, containing these old coins. On learning about this, people gather around him and want to have their share in that treasure. They harass him and take him to the city centre. A crowd gathers while that youth looks for some acquaintance, though to no avail. The church father interrogates him and he recounts his story. He asks those present to accompany him to that cave and meet his other friends. On reaching there, they see the Inscription and they believe in his version. On entering the cave they meet his friends who are alive, with halo and tranquility writ large on their faces. The report reaches the emperor Theodosius who visits the cave. Maximilan or Achilides declares that Allah put them to sleep and woke them up before the Last Day in order to prove the doctrine of Life after Death. Then those youths died and a place of worship was constructed there as memorial.[3]

As to the importance of this story in history, its authenticity is upheld by the leading historians and others and they do not regard it as improbable. All the classical books consistently report it, especially in the Christian world. Gibbon generally dismisses out of hand any supernatural story. However, regarding the Seven Sleepers he states:

This strange story cannot be equated with any Greek mythological story or folklore or their dogma. For, the authenticity of this report is on record for the next 50 years consistently. A Syrian Father, who was born two years after Theodosius, named James of Sarug has recorded this story in adulation of these youths of Ephesus at the end of sixth century. Gregory of Tours rendered this Syriac report into Latin. In the Eastern Christendom the People of the Cave were commemorated with reverence. Their names figure prominently in the Roman annals and festivals. Their fame was not confined to only Christendom.[4]

As to the number of years spent by them in the cave, it ranges from 300 to 307 years, as cited by some *mufassirun* (exegetes) on the authority of Christians, and in the *Encyclopaedia of Religion and Ethics*. The Qur'an speaks of 309 years. Classical *tafsir* writers ascribe the difference to the variation between the Gregorian and lunar calendars.

According to Ibn Kathir, Allah informed the Prophet (peace be upon him) of the period of their stay in the cave. They were woken up after their long sleep by Allah and then Allah let everyone (now about them. The period was 300 years. In the lunar calendar it

---

[3] See the article, "Seven Sleepers" in *Encyclopedia of Religion and Ethics*. The same story has been reported by Ibn Jarir Tabari and other *tafsir* scholars on the authority of Muhammad ibn Ishaq. However, owing to the absence of their access to Christian sources and ignorance of the pre-Christian Roman history, their account is marred by ambivalence. (For example, see *Tafsir Ibn Kathir*, 15: 123-126. We have therefore relied on the original Christian sources).

[4] Gibbon, "Seven Sleepers" in his *Decline and Fall of the Roman Empire*, 243-244.

is equivalent to 309 years. For lunar calendar gets behind the Gregorian calendar by 3 years in every 100 years. That is why the Qur'an says: "And added nine years."[5]

Common to the above quoted passages from Gibbon, *Encyclopaedia* and the account in books on history and *tafsir* is the point that this incident of hiding inside a cave happened during the reign of Decius, popularly known as Daqyanus in the Arabic sources. He was notorious for his intolerance, persecution and prejudice. Another version is that the appearance of the People of the Cave happened in the days of the believing king Theodosius II. The intervening period between the two kings is only 200 years and hence it poses a challenge. This also explains Gibbon's jibe at the duration of their sleep, mentioned in the Qur'an. Some classical and recent *tafsir* scholars[6] have tried to suggest a way out by asserting that the Qur'anic statement about their 309 years' sleep is a quotation from the people of the Book, not a Qur'anic assertion. The Qur'an reproduces their speculations about the issue. It is not a definitive statement. It should be read in conjunction with the preceding verses which cite the version of the people of the Book that they were three while the fourth one was their dog. They cite in this context the following verse, implying that Allah did not specify this period. Rather, the whole issue should be referred to Allah's knowledge. This is the stance of 'Abdullah ibn 'Abbas. However, 'Allamah Alusi points out that this report is on the authority of Hibr[7] who speaks of seven youths in the cave. In the next verse,[8] however, it is asserted that Allah knows best their number. So he could not take that stance.[9]

Some other scholars too, have not upheld the above stance, for it does not fit in with the Arabic idiom. For one would not instinctively reach the above conclusion. Imam Razi opines:

"It emerges from the relevant verses that there is no preceding

---

[5] *Tafsir Ibn Kathir*, Surah Al-Kahf.
[6] 'Allamah Jamaluddin Qasimi, *Tafsir Qāsimi*.
[7] It is the title of Ibn 'Abbas.
[8] Al-Kahf 18:22.
[9] *Ruh al-Ma'āni*, Tafsir Surah Al-Kahf.

statement. The message is loud and clear. While discarding what the people of the Book say, one should believe in the information provided by Allah."[10]

Shaykh Al-Islam Ibn Taimiyyah, while discussing the stance of the people of the Book, clarifies that the Qur'an states its own stance on the issue. It does not attribute anything to the people of the Book.[11]

Let us bring to mind the point about the divergence in the number of years provided by Gibbon and the Qur'an[12].

The crucial point to be addressed is the popular report that these youths had retired to a cave during the reign of Decius who had ruled from September 249 to June 251. He is notorious for his brutality, bloodshed, and persecution of Christians, insistence on offerings and animal sacrifice for idols.[13] Let us not lose sight of the fact that Decius had been on the throne for a short time, of less than two years.

Even this period was consumed by his war against the Goths. It was at their hands that he was Killed beside the river Rhine. It is doubtful that during this brief period he may have visited any eastern Christendom town. There is nothing on record about his travel to Greece or the eastern Christendom. It is mentioned in the *Historians' History of the World* that Decius's reign was too brief. After assuming office he had to quell a revolt and all of his time was spent on fighting against the Goths.

Historians have named the Christian leaders punished by him for defying the royal decree. They make no mention of the people of the Cave. Only a few Christians had been persecuted. According to Gibbon, their number was 10 men and 7 women.[14]

Moreover, the disappearance of a few Christians was a local issue. It was not so important as to draw the attention of historians

---

[10] *Tafsir* al-*Kabir,* Tafsir Surah Al-Kahf.

[11] *Al-Jawāb al-Sahih.*

[12] Ibid., 6: 413.

[13] The article, "Decius" in the *Encyclopaedia Britainnica,* 1968 Edition, 1, 157. It is common knowledge that this practice was initiated by Trajan, not Decius. During his reign the leading Church Fathers of Jerusalem and Aleppo were executed for their crime of professing Christianity. See George H. Dyer, *History of the Christian Church,* 6: 65-66.

[14] Gibbon, *History of the Decline and Fall of the Roman Empire,* 2: 98.

or writers. In comparison, their getting up after having slept for hundreds of years and their reception by clergy were reported everywhere in that it was something amazing. So their awakening during Theodosius's reign came to everyone's knowledge and it was reported everywhere. Historians have vied with one another in reporting it. It is therefore more likely that they were persecuted during the reign of the emperor Aelius Hadrian[15] who had ruled for a long time from 129 to 134. He had visited the eastern Christendom. It is not on record that he had actively persecuted those youths. He may not be even aware of this incident. By then the frontiers of the Roman Empire had expanded much and Roman officials were posted in far off towns. It is likely that some official may have indulged in persecution at the local level or may have tried to suppress the new religion, Christianity, in his own capacity out of his religious fervour or his desire to please his superiors. Such incidents do happen in every era. So if we assume that these youths had disappeared during Hadrian's reign and woke up in the days of Theodosius, the Christian and Qur'anic accounts may be easily reconciled, leaving out a minor difference of only a few years. This demolishes the ground on which Gibbon doubted

---

[15] Hadrian reigned between 117 and 138, succeeding Trajan. The Council ratified his ascension to the throne in August 117. He tried his level best to revive the glory of the old Greek towns and built a moat for protecting the Roman borders. He controlled the Jewish rebellion in 132 and in doing so he dealt with the rebels harshly and mercilessly. He ordered the exile of all Jews and let them visit Jerusalem only once a year. This institutionalized the expulsion and exile of Jews. (*The Historians' History of the World*). In 129 he toured Asia Minor and Syria and held his court at Smyrna, to which all the kings and nobles of the Eastern countries were invited. He spent winter at Aleppo and moved towards the south in 130. He ordered that a new town be built on the ruins of Al-Quds. After crossing the countries in Arabia he reached Egypt. In 133 he was forced into returning to Palestine in order to quell the Jewish revolt. He delegated his authority to Julius Severus and returned to Rome. At Baiae he died on 10 June 138. Combined in his personality were diverse strands. (*Encyclopaedia Britainnica*, Vol 11). George H. Dyer, a church historian sums up his personality thus: "Hadrian was no old Roman, but a modern spirit, curious, religious and skeptical. He maintained Trajan's policy in compelling heretics and atheists, mostly Christians to present offerings before idols and to be associated with the polytheistic Roman religion but cautioned against wholesale accusations." (*A History of Christian Church*, New York, 1896, 66).

the chronology of this event. The above version is plausible because the starting and concluding dates of the event are not precisely clear. There is much divergence of opinion among the Greek and Syrian historians on the year in which these youths had woken up. The latter place it in 425 or 437 while the former in 446,[16] in the 38th year of Theodosius's reign.[17]

It is our conviction that the Qur'an is the custodian of the earlier Scriptures and a more reliable source than the divergent reports which have been subject to accretion, deletion and corruption. During the reign of Nero (64 CE) there was an intense anti-Christianity wave and it lasted with its disastrous effects for long. At long last the Romans put an end to this trend in general. For in the 4th century Constantine accepted Christianity. Yet the history of Christianity is shrouded in uncertainty and doubt. Nothing definite can be said owing to weak reports. The historiography of the era is inaccurate. So there is deficit of trust.

A small group going into hiding in a small town has nothing dramatic to draw attention at the national level. However, their return after a long time was a major event, abounding in wonder and fervour, especially at a time when their co-religionist Christian emperor was on the throne.

The importance of this event may be better appreciated against the backdrop of the controversy raging then about the Resurrection and the Life-after-Death. Some were deadly opposed to these doctrines. For long a need had been felt for some clear evidence to establish the veracity of this belief. It was then that the People of the cave woke up and their account reached everywhere. It cleared all doubts. Man is naturally drawn towards something unusual or fanciful. He records such reports more fervently. So religious, emotional and rational grounds were there for recording and transmitting this event to future generations. The starting point of this event lacked any mass appeal. Nor was there any drive to document it. And Allah knows truth best.

---

[16] See Gibbon's *History*.
[17] Theodosius ruled from 408 to 450.

Why the Qur'an takes up this story?

According to the Qur'anic scholars, the circumstantial setting of this story in the Qur'an is contained in the report narrated by Muhammad ibn Ishaq's following report.[18] A delegation of Quraysh went to the Jewish rabbis to get some questions which would help them check the veracity of the Prophet's claim to be the Messenger of Allah. Accordingly, they gave some questions, of which one pertained to the People of the Cave.

---

[18] According to Ibn Jarir, "This report is on the authority of Abu Kuraib, Yunus ibn Bakr and Muhammad ibn Ishaq, an Egyptian shaykh who was more than 40 years old, 'Ikrimah and Ibn 'Abbas that Quraysh deputed Nasr ibn Al-Harith and 'Uqbah ibn Abi Mu'it to the Jewish rabbis in order to seek their opinion about Prophet Muhammad (peace be upon him). They should apprise them of his sayings and character. For these rabbis are from the people of the Book and possess more Prophetic knowledge than us. When they reached Madina, they asked the rabbis about the Prophet (peace be upon him) and told them about his character and sayings. They told them: "You are the scholars of the Torah. We have contacted you. Please inform us about him." The Jewish rabbis replied: "Ask him the three question which we tell you. If he is a Messenger sent down by Allah, he will answer these correctly. If he is unable to reply, you should know that he is an impostor and then take a suitable action. Ask him about the youths who had disappeared a long time ago. For theirs is an amazing story. Ask him about a globetrotter who had reached both the East and the West. Ask him to relate to you his story. And ask him as to what is the true nature of soul. If he answers these questions and recounts to you all relevant details, you should follow the Prophet (peace be upon him). If he does not say anything, (now that he invents false ideas." Both of them returned to Makkah and told Quraysh: "We have brought to you something decisive, of which the Jewish scholars have informed us. Then they recounted those questions. He told them that he would reply the next day. They went to Prophet Muhammad (peace be upon him) and asked him to respond. While saying this he did not utter *Inshā-Allah.* (Allah willing) For the next 15 days he did not receive any revelation. Nor did Jibril visit him. This gave an opportunity to the unbelievers to mock and criticize him. For he had promised to reply the next day. They mocked as to why revelation was not sent to him. The Prophet (peace be upon him) was hurt by their taunting. It was then that Jibril brought him Surah Al-Kahf. He was chided for his grieving over the matter. The Surah contained an account of those youths, that glob-trotter and the soul. Let this be realized that one of the narrators of this report is obscure on whose authority Muhammad ibn Ishaq has narrated this report. According to the norms of *hadith* methodology, it is not a very reliable report.

Even if it is an authentic report, it cannot be regarded as the sole reason behind recounting this story in the Qur'an. For there had been many more instances of persecution which could be ascertained only through revelation. The Qur'anic scholars have discussed at length the reports which state as to why a particular Qur'anic verse was revealed. Classical scholars paid much attention to those reports. However, these are not so important as held by many scholars. Actually, the Qur'an has been sent down for guidance and reform. It was revealed in Prophet Muhammad's day when degeneration was at its height. However, the Qur'an addresses all generations of mankind and there has not been any essential difference in the human nature. Therefore, some questions representing the desire of some persons for a trial are not that important. In his valuable book *Al-Fawz al-Kabir*, Shah Waliyullah draws attention to the following truth:

The *mufassirin* in general ascribe a verse containing a command to an event, taking as the cause behind its revelation. It is a truism that the Qur'an has been revealed basically for reforming man and for eliminating false beliefs and evil deeds. Therefore the presence of false beliefs in any group is a sufficient reason for the revelation of Qur'anic verses and commands. The verses which admonish man are occasioned by the incidence of evil deeds, wrongdoings and negligence. Qur'anic commands, Allah's bounties and signs and exemplary events recur in the Qur'an. The Qur'anic scholars have gone to great lengths in relating some events as the cause of revelation. This is not really so. Only such verses are an exception which speak of any particular incident in Prophet Muhammad's day or earlier. For informing readers better, the allusion may be explained.[19]

The story of the People of the Cave is placed aptly and in a suitable context and time. For the Muslims in Makkah at that time had been confronting similar circumstances which these youths had to face at the hands of the oppressive rulers.

Their life had been identical with that of those believing youths before they went into hiding. The Qur'an presents a graphic picture

---

[19] *Al-Fawz al-Kabir.*

of the plight of the Makkan Muslims:

> Recall that you were few in number and were considered as
> weak in the land. You feared that men might do away with
> you.
>
> (8: 26)

The persecution of Muslims in the day is recorded in *hadith* collections and works on *sirah* (Prophet Muhammad's life). These contain the heart-wrenching plight of Bilal, 'Ammar, Mus'ab, Sumaiyyah and their Companions. One feels revulsion towards the account of their persecution. The Qur'an and *sirah* works depict the suffocating atmosphere of the day in which these Makkan Muslims led their lives.

There was no ray of hope in the all-enveloping darkness. Nor was there any whiff of breeze in the choking conditions. Muslims had been in a cleft stick, struggling in the claws of a beast. The Qur'an projects their condition thus:

> They felt so guilty over their staying a home that the earth
> despite being vast seemed narrow to them. Their own lives
> became at burden to them. They realised that there is no
> escape from Allah. He alone can give them refuge.
>
> (9: 118)

It was then that they were blessed by revelation (*wahy*). The Qur'an recounted to them an account detailing how hardship makes way for ease, and how humiliation is replaced by honour and glory and divine help in a miraculous fashion. What happened to these youths was beyond any speculation and challenged all rational categories. It became common knowledge that Allah delivered a handful of youths who were resourceless. Yet they overcame the forces of unbelief and persecution. Since Allah enjoys all power, wealth and resources, He brings forth the dead from the living, and the living from the dead, and lets light appear from the depths of darkness. Allah transformed the bloodthirsty killers, who had been after the blood of people into carers and custodians. Allah makes a believing son an heir to an unbelieving father.

Similarity between the Makkan believers and the People of the Cave

In the all-round depressing conditions with hardships looming everywhere, the Qur'an reminded the early Muslims of the instructive stories of Prophet Yusuf (peace be upon him) and his brothers, and of Prophet Musa and Harun (peace be upon them). These recount the encounter between individuals and groups, and a Prophet and his community. The story under discussion, of the clash between an oppressive king and the devout believers, states how faith works. The Makkan Muslims and the People of the Cave stand out different in their era, ethos, personalities and other details. However, in the final analysis they are identical. Common to both is the role of Allah's absolute power that prevails over everyone, be he a believer or unbeliever, pious or evil, victim or wrongdoer, the weak or the strong and the rich or the poor. He makes one triumphant in a way that cannot be rationally explained. It forces even an unbeliever to embrace faith, as it leaves no doubt. Allah says at the conclusion of Surah Yusuf:

> There is a great lesson in these accounts for the people gifted with understanding. The Qur'an is not something invented or false. It confirms earlier revelations and explains everything. It is guidance and mercy for the believing people.
>
> (12: 111)

Likewise, Surah Hud ends at this note:

> Allah relates to you (O Prophet) the account of the Messengers. This will make your heart strong. In this is the truth, advice and reminder for the believers.
>
> (11: 120)

On studying the conditions of the Makkan Muslims one realises the commonalities between them and the People of the Cave. For defending their faith the latter had left their home town and taken refuge in a mountain cave. They stayed inside it for a long time until the hostile state that had been persecuting them collapsed. And after the long rule of idolatrous and wrongdoing Roman rule, Theodosius acceded to the throne who was a supporter of Christianity. He took pride in his Christian credentials. He intended to honour all those who had been persecuted and glorified them as they deserved it.

Likewise, the Makkan Muslims resolutely adhered to their faith, though they suffered much. Eventually their deliverance was facilitated by migration (*hijrat*). They took refuge in a stronger and more secure place, *Yathrib* (Madinah) than that cave. Allah did them more favours than which He had bestowed upon the People of the Cave who had hidden themselves in a cave in the second century. Allah decreed that His religion may prevail over all others through these Muslims, not leaving out any part of the world:

> It is Allah Who sent His Messenger with guidance and true faith that He may make it prevail over all other religions, no matter how much the polytheists may dislike it.
>
> (61:9)

Allah sent down Prophet Muhammad (peace be upon him) and his advent marked the conclusion of the institution of Prophethood and through Prophet Muhammad (peace be upon him) the Muslim community was evolved.

> (O believers), you are the best community evolved for mankind. You command good and forbid evil, and you believe in Allah.
>
> (3: 110)

Prophet Muhammad (peace be upon him) is on record, exhorting Muslims) "You have been sent to facilitate things, not to complicate things."[20]

---

[20] Narrated by Abu Hurayrah.

For this Muslim minority a cave was insufficient. They could not lead life while being cut off from all else. They were entrusted with preaching Islam. The future of mankind rested on them. They were the best of creation, or in the words of Prophet Jesus (peace be upon him) the salt of the earth. They could bring about greenery everywhere, promising a bright future for mankind. Allah did not want them to go wayward. They were not to lead an ascetic's life. Rather, it was their job to preach Islam openly and publicly, to challenge falsehood actively and to free mankind from wrongdoing and oppression. They were to uphold the name of Allah and to make His word prevail over all else:

> Fight against them until the mischief is over. Let justice and faith in Allah prevail fully and everywhere.

(8: 39)

When one of the youths went out of the cave after sleep, he witnessed a totally new spectacle) the people, culture, civilization and religion had changed altogether. Their own religion was now supreme and their beliefs were respected.

Likewise, when the *Muhājirin* from Madinah returned to Makkah, the locals warmly received them. Islam was now dominant in Makkah. The Ka'bah key was in Prophet Muhammad's hand and he was free to entrust it to him whom he liked. Islam stood for honour and glory whereas polytheism and idolatry were discredited. Those who had been expelled from Makkah were now the rulers, teachers of mankind and guide to the entire humanity.

Viewed thus, the story of the People of the Cave had a striking resemblance with the state of believers and young *Muhājirin*. The minor differences were on account of the temperament of Islam and the constant change which marks man's life.

History repeating itself

Allah has decreed public promotion of Islam and continuation of the Muslim community. It is therefore inevitable that they undergo the same trials which other communities had faced. Its call will take on the forces of unbelief. At times it had the upper hand and at others, it faced losses. They were in both majority and minority and faced support or hardship. We have often noted that the groups standing for truth undergo very hard tests. They had to face physical torture and exile. This is perpetrated by both non-Muslims and the so-called Muslim states. The latter even pledges its loyalty to Islam, builds mosques, organises Islamic religious programmes and celebrates Eid on a grand scale. However, these so-called Islamic states regard the call to Islam based on sound articles of faith as more pernicious than any *Jāhiliyyah* movement, polytheistic notion and atheism. In such a situation the story of the People of the Cave is re-enacted. A clash erupts between a tiny minority of believers and the huge majority comprising hypocrites and the Muslim youths derive inspiration from the example of the People of the Cave:

> (O Prophet), "We tell you their account in truth. They were the youths who had believed in their Lord. We increased them in guidance. We made their hearts strong."
> They stood up and declared: "O our Lord, You are the Lord of the heavens and the earth. We will not worship any god besides You. If we do so, it will be blasphemy."
>
> (18: 13-14)

At times, this ordeal is so tough that it is quite a task to survive while keeping faith intact. The only option for Muslims then is to migrate. This has been happening down the ages at intervals. However, Prophet Muhammad's illustrious career is the source of guidance in every era. It identifies such situations, as Prophet Muhammad (peace be upon him) remarked: "It is likely that a believer may be left with only his goats and for defending his faith he may retire to a mountain or a fertile valley along with these."[21]

Surah Al-Kahf provides guidance when faced with this challenge and shows him the straight way which is to be followed.

Let us now study the story of the People of the Cave as presented in the Qur'an. It projects an almost live account of characters and abounds in lessons for us.

The idolatrous and Epicurean society in Ephesus, Rome

Ephesus, a town in the Roman Empire, represented the nadir of materialism and epicureanism in the early year of Christianity. History informs us of the nexus between idolatry and sexual promiscuity, as if there exists a secret pact between the two. This point is borne out also by the history and ruins of the ancient India, Egypt, Greece and Arabia. The same appeared to be at work in Ephesus in the Roman Empire. Under the sway of idolatry and sexual degeneration, moral and spiritual values had lost their lustre and control. There flourished a grossly materialistic society in the heart of the Roman Empire which placed premium only on appearances, pleasures of the flesh and short, temporary gains. The state exercised its total control over all resources. It accounted for people's prosperity, honour and well-being. Following the dictates of state was an easy way to attain all material gains and secure an honourable position. As a result, the self-seekers and opportunists thronged the court. People were given to their base desires who were crazy about worldly positions and wealth.

The state was bent upon imposing its ideology upon public. It persecuted anyone who opposed its unbridled, idolatrous way of life and deprived him of life and property and civil liberties. The entire country was forced into following a particular way of life, of which superstitions and base desires were the main components. It had no room for any diversity in terms of faith and morals. All citizens, irrespective of the difference in class, age and mental level were reduced only to be the photocopies of the original prescribed by state, without any addition or deletion.

---

[21] Narrated by Abu Said Khudri (*Bukhāri*).

Radical believers

In this idolatrous, oppressive, degenerate and regimented society reeking of suffocation there were some persons who greeted the call to Christianity, for they were tender hearted, conscientious and, sane and sensible persons. This call overwhelmed them and they were fired by their faith and conviction. For them it was inconceivable to lead life without faith. They were not ready to abandon their faith for even a fabulous price and pledged to lay down their lives for defending their faith.

So this is how the struggle ensued. At first, they felt this conflict, deep into their heart and later in other domains. This is a truism that one feels this discontent first in his heart. They took to a path parallel to that of state. The idolatrous state did not entertain any diversity. The society was steeped in evil and could not tolerate anything other than evil. It was hard to lead life without toeing the line drawn by state and society. The ethos, socio-cultural forces and the grim ground realities forced them to surrender to state. For they could not otherwise survive. They were denied food and money. All worldly positions were under state control. They could not flourish without state patronage. They could buy peace, security and happiness only by reconciling with their society and state. The only option was opportunism and to follow the prevalent thought patterns and public opinion. This materialistic line of reasoning appeals to the human mind and this mindset is fairly common.

However, these believers defied the above logic. They sought inspiration and strength from their faith. For the supporters of evil, however, following the popular trend is the only way out. These believers foresaw the distant future and rejected the present exigencies. For them, the model was different, away from the present. They could perceive the Supreme Power beyond and above the means deployed by state and society. Allah's will is the overwhelming cause in that He has created all causes. His will accounts for the working of the universe. Those patronized by Him are not bound by cause and effect. Allah facilitates things for them and their era instead of dictating terms to them follows in their footsteps. He makes thing easy and pleasant for them and lavished upon them His special mercy. So they did not have to surrender themselves to material resources and bowing down before anyone. They did not have to humiliate themselves by begging someone for help.

At this stage faith triumphed over materialism and the logic of faith prevailed. This essential message of the Surah features thus in the Qur'an:

> (O Prophet), "We tell you their account in truth. They were the youths who had believed in their Lord. We increased them in guidance. We made their hearts strong."
>
> They stood up and declared) "O our Lord, You are the Lord of the heavens and the earth. We will not worship any god besides You. If we do so, it will be blasphemy.
>
> Our community has taken gods besides Allah. They do not, however, have any proof for this. Who is a greater wrongdoer than he who invents a lie against Allah?"

(18: 13-15)

Life without faith or faith without life

However, the big question was how to adhere to faith when under the influence of state the whole population was hostile; all avenues of income were blocked and life was made difficult for them. They could opt for a life without faith or such faith that lacked life.

At this juncture they were guided by faith as their hearts were blessed with the conviction that Allah's land is vast and that they should rely on His help and support. Since they had already renounced all pleasures and joys of life, they were not obliged to be stuck at one place:

(They talked among themselves): "As you have turned away from them and their gods, go to a cave for shelter. Your Lord will extend you His mercy and will decide your case in your favour."

(18:16)

When to leave home for faith

They could move in any direction, and each of them could go his own way and lead his own life. Or each one of them could retire to a cave or a mountain peak, as was the practice of Christians in their ascetic life in the day. However, Allah inspired them to leave town together and while being faithful to their beliefs and seeking Allah's mercy, help and support, they should behave like true believers. They had no other option, as all doors were closed on them and there lurked a serious threat to their faith.

Reward for conviction, fortitude and migration in the cause of Allah

As they fulfilled the requisites of faith and resolve, which are essential for securing Allah's help and support, these youths who had believed in Allah, found that Allah fulfilled His promise to them. He increased them in guidance and fortitude:

We increased them in guidance. We made their hearts strong.

(18:13-14)

A Muslim migrant, who rises in revolt against his society and oppressive state, needs most consistency and guidance. He stands in need of peace and tranquility for his anxious, disturbed heart, to be provided by Allah. In the case of these believing, pious youths Allah fulfilled His promise, and blessed them with more guidance, boosted their morale and substituted cowardice, fear and anxiety with fortitude, tranquility strength, confidence ecstasy and self-surrender to Allah. This is the bulwark for every migrant in Allah's cause who revolts against the Godless society and his times.

As they left their town, away from the charms of their society, culture and economy, and more importantly, their hearth and home, including their dear and noble family members,[22] Allah guided them to a cave,[23] which was most appropriate from the viewpoint of health.[24] Even big organizations could not construct such a spacious, suitable refuge. For it did receive the sunlight and warmth yet it was safe again excessive heat. They were provided with fresh, life- giving air:

> When the sun rose, it moved away from their cave to the right. When it set, it moved away to the left. They were in the open space in the middle of the cave.
>
> (18: 17)

This put an end to their link with their impure, evil surroundings and culture and its wicked, wrongdoing votaries forever. They developed their direct link with nature. They were cut off from the outside world yet they kept benefitting from its valuable gains. It was the fruit of their invincible, true faith and represented Allah's favour and guidance:

> This was one of the signs of Allah. He whom Allah guides is on guidance.
>
> (18: 17)

Those opposed to Allah's creative power, shari'ah and nature have

---

[22] According to 'Allamah Alusi, these youths hailed from the families of the nobles and aristocrats. (*Ruh al-Ma'āni*, 5: 11.)

[23] According to *Lisān al-'Arab*, *Al-Kahf* is used of a big cave in a mountain. *Al-Maghārah* is employed for a small cave.

[24] Surah Al-Kahf 18: 17. It is explained in *Ruh al-Ma'āni* that these youths were not exposed to the sunlight which could cause them inconvenience. They were in the middle of the cave, had a constant supply of fresh air and they were safe against the intense heat of the sunlight inside that cave. (5: 20) Imam Razi points out that the mouth of the cave was to the north hence when the sun rose, it was to the right of the cave and at sunset to its north. (5: 466).

exhausted their talent, time and energy, and also their knowledge and mental process on securing long life. For this they have tapped forces of nature and invented all sorts of comfort and luxury. However, they have been unsuccessful in discovering the elixir of life. Their efforts have been to no avail and they have turned into victims of their own inventions, fatal diseases, complex problems and disastrous wars:

> He whom He misleads, you will not find any helper to lead him to the straight way.
>
> (18:17)

Life of the Faithful in the Cave

They did not lead the life of inaction in the cave. They were not subject to aimlessness or darkness. For they were not without Allah's guidance. It appears that they had carried with them some scrolls related to the Torah and the Gospels and teachings of Prophets, when they left town.[25]

This model should be followed by all migrants in the cause of faith, when migration is the only option.

When their provisions which they had carried were exhausted, Allah put them to deep sleep which made them indifferent to food and drink:

---

[25] The Qur'an speaks together of the people of the Cave and the Inscription. The latter have been identified variously by *tafsir* writers. For some it signifies only the stone tablet on which their story or names were inscribed and it was installed at the mouth of the cave. For some *al-raqeem* was the name of that village or town. In his article Gilani opines that the reference is to the scrolls which these youths had with them in that cave. This view is supported by the report cited by the author of *Ruh al-Maʿāni* on the authority of Abdullah ibn Abbas that they carried a book containing the Christian teachings. (5:11). We prefer this version. Ibn Jabir quotes Ibn Zayd to the effect: "*Raqeem* stands for a book. Allah has kept the identity of this book a secret." Then he recited verses 19-21 of Surah Al-Mutafiffin. Imam Bukhari also identifies *raqeem* with a book.

So Allah made them sleep in the cave for a number of years.

(18: 11)

Transformation of the Roman Empire

Another big miracle happened related to the People of the Cave. During the long period of their sleep and exile, their town, rather the entire Roman Empire underwent a major change. Idolatry and promiscuity and their votaries became a thing of past, as they were forgotten without a trace. On the debris of that idolatrous and degenerate society there emerged a new government and state that believed in Allah and Prophet 'Isa (peace be upon him).[26] The rulers embraced Christianity against which they had been at war for ages. They used to persecute and exile Christians. Now the very same Christians were respected and honoured. At that time these youths woke up, ending their sleep which had lasted for more than 300 years:

They stayed in their cave for three hundred years. Others add nine more years to it.

(18:25)

They asked one another as to how long they had slept and they expressed different views on this issue. Then they left this matter to Allah, for such points are not so important in this life or the Next:

---

[26] This happened during the reign of Constantine the Great. He had taken over the reins of power in 306 and according to a popular report he had embraced Christianity. (Many historians doubt the sincerity and integrity of this move. For them he did so for political expediency). He declared Christianity as state religion. He convened several synods (religious councils) for reconciling the differences among Christian sects and dissensions. He laid the foundations of the town known as Constantinople, which was his capital. He died in 337.

One of them asked: "How long did you stay here?" Some of them replied) "We stayed for a day or part of a day." Finally they said: "Your Lord knows best how long you stayed here."

(18: 19)

After some time, they feel hungry and ask one of their companions to arrange for clean, wholesome food.[27] He goes to town, carrying silver coins of their days:

> Now send one of you with your coin to the town. Let him find
> out which is the best food and let him bring some to you.

(18: 19)

They thought that the rulers were still hostile to them and state spies had been watching them. That is why they had asked their companion to conduct himself tactfully in town:

> "Let him be careful and not inform anyone about you. For if
> they (the unbelieving people of the town) find about you, they
> will stone you to death or force you to return to their faith. If
> this happens, you will never get success."

(18: 19-20)

The local people were familiar with the history of these youth how during the era of the idolatrous rulers they had been persecuted. They knew about their sudden disappearance. The new Christian state intended to establish its Christian credentials, glorify its heroes and martyrs and set up a memorial commemorating the People of the Cave and the Inscription.

---

[27] Imam Razi explains *azka ta'ām* as wholesome, delicious food. He adds that this verse instructs us to carry provisions for a journey. The shari'ah ordains it and this arrangement does not run counter to one's belief in trust in Allah.

41

The exiles turn into heroes

The story of the People of the Cave became the talk of the town. That youth moved carefully as he wanted to return at the earliest along with food to his friends. However, he now became the centre of attention as he and other youths were declared heroes. Their resilience and heroism was glorified by both state and the general public.

The secret came into light by the silver coins, dress and accent of that youth. The Qur'an does not delve into such details. For guidance is its main concern, not the story in itself. The story of these youths spread far and wide in no time across the country. It was discussed by one and all. People thronged to the cave where they had sheltered. The Qur'an avoids all the details about their reception. However, it declares forcefully:

> Thus, Allah let the people recognize that Allah's promise is true and that there is no doubt about the Last Day (and raising after death).
>
> (18: 21)

The transformation of both state and people and the appearance of these youths after their long absence represent the fulfilment of Allah's promise for preserving their striving and for annihilating their enemy. It underscores the truth that the alternation of day and night and the rise and fall of people are in Allah's hands:

> There is no doubt that the Last Day is coming. Allah will bring back to life those who are in graves.
>
> (22: 7)

No one could then expect the end of that oppressive rule, revival of Christianity, emergence of those youths from that Cave (which was no less than their tomb) their glorification and warm reception by state and the general public. Did it not contain a loud and clear message for the Quraysh and Makkan chiefs and for the weak, oppressed Muslims? It had a lesson for the former and hope and comfort for the latter. These youths lived as long as Allah willed and then died. Their admirers differed on the form of a suitable memorial for them:

> They had differences about the people of the Cave. Some of them suggested: "Construct a building over their cave (as a memorial)." Their Lord knows best about them. Those in charge of their affair decided to build a place of worship over their cave.

(18: 21)[28]

This warm reception and memorial were not confined to only that time. They stand immortalized in the annals of history and religion. Various groups have interpreted their contribution differently. They have been nonetheless dear to all:

> Some say they were three while the fourth one was their dog. Some hold that they were five while the sixth one was their dog. All this is only guess work. Some say that they were seven while the eighth one was their dog. (O Prophet), say) "My Lord alone knows best their number. Only a few (now their correct number. Do not dispute any more about their number. Follow only that matter which is clear. Do not ask anyone about them."

(18: 22)

---

[28] Surah Al-Kahf 18: 21. While explicating this verse 'Allamah Alusi says: "Some cite this verse to justify erecting structures over the graves of saints and use it as a mosque. This notion does not hold any water and is absolutely false. Bukhari, and Muslim and Nasa'i cite A'ishah, and Abu Hurayrah, as quoted by Muslim, report: "Allah's curse be on Jews and Christians who turned the graves of their Prophets into places of worship." Ahmad and Nasa'i add that these people will be the worst creatures in the Hereafter. The verse only refers to this plan by some persons. Their view is not endorsed or presented as a model. It is hard to identify as to who had made this suggestion. Hence their suggestion is not binding to follow. It is speculated that this suggestion was given by the rulers and nobility, as is implied by Qatadah." (*Ruh al- Ma'āni*, 5: 31-32).

Triumph of Faith over Materialism

This marks the end of the amazing story of the People of the Cave in Surah Al-Kahf which recounts the clash between Materialism and Faith. It is about the trust or its lack in the Creator of causes. This story concludes with the triumph of Faith over materialism and trust in the Creator of causes and reliance on Him.

These true believing youths preferred faith to materialism, and the eternal gains of the Hereafter to the short-term benefits of this life. They liked more to lead a destitute's life while maintaining their faith, rather than amassing wealth and abandoning their faith. They decided to leave their home, family and friends in preference to indulging in the pleasures of the flesh and enjoying worldly power and honour. They dismissed any idea of gratifying their base desires and colluding with sin, rebellion and wrong doing. They paid more attention to the dictates of faith, rather than to the joys of this life. They devoted themselves heart and soul to spirituality. It turned out later that they were more far-sighted, meticulous and discerning. For the pious have an excellent end. They were drawn more to the Creator of causes than to causes and weathered all hardships in this cause. Eventually, material causes supported them and the state which had earlier persecuted them, honoured them. The account of the People of the Cave underscores their fortitude, consistency, resolve, *jihād* and self-sacrifice. This conflict recurs in history, especially of Faith. It proves that causes are subservient to Allah's will and these affirm good conduct. It is the job of believers to pursue the way of Faith and good deeds in order to win Allah's pleasure, help and support.

Prior to recounting the story of the owner of the two gardens, the Qur'an exhorts Prophet Muhammad (peace be upon him) to adhere fast to Allah's rope. This is the way prescribed by Faith and the Qur'an. He is advised to ensure company with those believers who are fortunately blessed with Faith, gnosis, Allah's remembrance and supplications, even if they have little share in worldly goods. He should keep away from those ignorant and negligent people who are devoid of Faith, conviction, and gnosis and their effects such as mentioning and supplicating to Allah, even though they may have an abundance of worldly goods.

The above exhortation is of general import, directed at everyone who recites and believes in the Qur'an. Believers should pay special heed to it and they need to act upon it:

> Keep yourself content in the company of those who call their Lord morning and evening. They want His pleasure alone. Do not neglect them, seeking the glitter of the life of this world. Do not follow him whose heart Allah has made neglect His mention. He follows only his desires. His case is of the one who has crossed the limits.
>
> (18: 28)

It has been the practice of the People of the Cave, believers and those having the gnosis of Allah to maintain a close spiritual link with Allah, adhere to Faith and be engaged in doing good. They prefer all this to materialism.

They have always arisen against the votaries of materialism.

They are never drawn towards worldliness and its charms.

This is the essential message of Surah Al-Kahf:

> Do not even look at the things of the life of this world which Allah has given for enjoyment to people. He tests them through these. Your Lord's blessing is the best and long lasting.
>
> (20: 131)

Materialism in *Dajjāl* culture and its glory

Materialistic culture (we can call its distinct form as *Dajjāl* culture) is opposed to the above message, or even inclination. It celebrates and glorifies the champions of materialism. Rather, it follows their way. Their literature, philosophy, poetry, prose, journalism, novel, drama, history and other corpus abound in praising, in a cringey way, capitalists, political powers and influential persons. They have deified their culture as something perfect and eternal and exhort everyone to fall in line.

Extremism in *Dajjāl* culture

The following verse depicts the mindset of this extremist and undiscerning culture and its proponents:

> Do not follow him whose heart Allah has made neglect His mention. He follows only his desires. His case is of the one who has crossed the limits.

(18: 28)

This culture is marred by extravagance, hyperbole and extremism. They betray extremism in both earning and spending money, in leisure and entertainment. The same extremism characterizes their political and economic concepts. They follow the same approach, in democracy and autocracy, and socialism. They abide by man-made laws and values. They do not deviate an inch from their own criteria. One transgressing the bounds set by them, in their opinion, does not deserve any honour or respect. Their rebellion runs counter to reason, good taste and human nature. For it places man in the category of beasts and cattle[29].

Faith stands for justice and moderation

The way of life prescribed by the Prophet (peace be upon him) is characterized by justice and moderation:

> They spend yet they neither waste nor act as misers. They follow the middle path.

(25: 67)

---

[29] This tendency is to the fore in the new movements in Europe and USA which promote animal like unbridled freedom, nudity and free sex, which are highly popular among the youth there, known as Hippies. This is the outcome of the culture which is soaked in materialism and produces frustration and depression. At some point in time similar conditions prevailed in Greece and Rome. On studying Plato's *Republic* one can gain a clear picture, for it records the mental make-up of the Greek youths. (For details see Sayyid Abul Hasan Ali Nadwi, *Rise and Fall of Islam: Its Impact on the Muslim World*).

Allah speaks of balance and moderation as the distinguishing mark of the community raised by the Qur'an.

> Allah has made you (O Muslims) a community of the middle way so that you might be witnesses to mankind and the Messenger be a witness to you.
>
> (2: 143)[30]

Prophet Muhammad (peace be upon him) was a perfect example of balance and moderation.[31] The Qur'an refers to the same as an outstanding trait of Islam. It is designated as *qayyim*. The Qur'an proclaims:

> (O Prophet), say) "My Lord has guided me to the straight way, the right religion. It is the way of Abraham who was true in faith. He was not of the polytheists."
>
> (6: 161)

> This is the straightway.
>
> (9: 36)

> Turn your face exclusively to true faith before there comes the Day from Allah which cannot be avoided.
>
> (30: 43)

The Qur'an is also termed as something balanced, which is free

---

[30] Al-Baqarah 2: 143. In *Madārik* it is stated: "As Allah has placed your *qiblah* (focal point for offering prayer) between the east and the west, He has kept you away from extremism." (p. 47) According to Khazin: "This verse means that Allah has made you bearers of a religion which shuns extremism." (1, 108).

[31] Prophet Muhammad's exemplary sense of moderation and balance in everything is evident from his sayings and teachings, as recorded in the works on *Sirah*. On this trait of the Prophet (peace be upon him), 'Ali ibn Abi Talib (RA) remarks: "He always acted moderately. He would never cross limits. On having a choice between two things, he always opted for the easier one." (*Tirmidhi, Shamāi'l*).

from any defect. Surah Al-Kahf opens thus:

> All praise belongs to Allah Who sent the Book to His servant. There is no defect in it. It is straight and clear. It warns against Allah's terrible punishment. It gives good news to the believers who do good that there is excellent reward for them. They will live in Paradise forever.

(18: 1-3)

The Qur'an also says:

> A Messenger from Allah, reciting from the pure pages of the Books, which are true.

(98: 2-3)

> This Arabic Qur'an is free from any defect. Let them fear (evil)!

(39: 28)

It goes without saying that truth and balance permeate the spirit of Islam, its laws, culture, and teachings. In contrast, the materialistic culture, which came into existence as a result of revolt against religion, has been devoid of balance. Its collective system is marred by extremism and its philosophy is flawed. Its literature is disfigured by hyperboles and a desire to take on a convoluted path. Given this, if this culture is bereft of balance, reason, truth and simplicity, it is not surprising.

Chapter 2

STORY OF THE OWNER OF THE TWO GARDENS

The Qur'an recounts the story of the owner of the two gardens. This story is more common than the story of the people of the Cave. If the latter happens once in centuries, the former is an everyday occurrence. It is the story of a fortunate person who was blessed in every respect. He had all the facilities available to him and had two grape vineyards, around which were date palm trees, with cornfields in between. It was the highest felicity imaginable for a middle class family. This is the standard of success and prosperity in the middle class. This man owed his prosperity to the means available to him. Both the gardens produced maximum harvest.

> Both the gardens gave full produce, without failure. Allah had caused a river to flow in the middle of the two.
>
> (18: 33)

Materialistic worldview and its narrowness

However, this person had the same materialistic mindset which is common to the ruling class, landlords, nationalist leaders, industrialists and military generals.

They are driven by their materialistic desires which are not bound by faith, sound understanding of Allah and moral training. He attributed his success and prosperity to his Knowledge, hard work, and mental process. The same was asserted by Qarun, as he said:

> However, Qarun said: "All this has been given to me because of a certain knowledge that I have."
>
> (28: 78)

He mocks his friend who was not blessed like him. With audacity he declares:

The owner had plenty of fruits. He said to his companion: "I have more wealth and more honour and greater following than you."

(18: 34)

He is so much engrossed in his wealth and power that he is aware of neither himself nor his Lord. Likewise, he has no inkling about divine causes and Allah's decree from the high above. His decree renders man's decision and wealth ineffective. He wrongs himself in terms of morals and reason. Being given to materiliasm he declares that no damage may befall him or his gardens. Nor will he suffer any loss in the Hereafter. He foolishly thinks that his success and prosperity are eternal and that he will enjoy it forever even in the Hereafter, if there is any:

While wronging himself he entered his garden and said: "I do not think this garden will ever perish. I do not think there ever will be the Last Day."

(18: 35-36)

He thinks that he is one of the select few who will be always blessed by good fortune and forever he will be on the top:

"I do not think there ever will be the Last Day. Even if I am returned to my Lord, I will get a better place."

(18: 36)

Persons with such mindset think that they do not have to care for faith and good deeds. Rather, what they acquire will always keep them happy.

The worldview of Faith

His friend was, by Allah's leave, receptive to truth and faith. He possessed the eternal wealth of gnosis and a good understanding of divine actions and attributes. He recognized that Allah alone runs this universe and is the Creator of causes. He may, whenever He wills so, change any situation altogether. He opposed his friend's materialistic viewpoint openly and apprised him of the truth which the materialists always disregard. Rather, they hate its mention:

Upon this his companion said: "Do you disbelieve in Him Who created you from clay? He created you out of a sperm drop and then shaped you as a human being."

(18: 37)

That arrogant person resented even hearing this. But his friend represented a totally different viewpoint. He had unquestioning faith in Allah:

However, I believe that Allah is my Lord. I do not take any partner with my Lord.

(18: 38)

He reminded him of the same truth which serves as the axis of Surah Al-Kahf. He diagnosed correctly his weakness, pointing out that means and causes are not the real thing. It is the Creator and Master Who has power over all means and causes. Someone may rejoice in what he has. But this is not owing to his own skills or mental accomplishments. Everything is because of only Allah's wisdom and power.

He has created everything in the best shape. Factfully, he draws his friend's attention to Allah's power and blessings:

When you entered your garden, why did not you say: "What Allah wills happens?" There is no power besides Allah.

(18: 39)

Spirit of this Surah and the key of this story

That "Allah does whatever He wills and there is no power besides Him" is the underlying message of this Surah. It provides the key to understanding this story. Allah exhorts Prophet Muhammad (peace be upon him) and all those reciting the Qur'an along with him to refer their matters and future plans to Him. He will decree as He wills:

> Do not say about anything) "I will do this tomorrow." Rather say: "(I will do this tomorrow) if Allah wills so." Bring to mind your Lord when you forget. Say: "I hope my Lord will guide me to the right direction."

(18: 23-24)

One should have this conviction that only that happens what Allah wills and He accomplishes all that He intends.

One who attributes every blessing and perfection to Allah, trusts Him while intending to do something and looks forward to His grace and mercy cannot join hands with those who believe only in external factors and materialism. He cannot be guided by them *Māshā Allah* and *Inshā-Allah*, the two brief expressions, are often used unconsciously, without bringing to mind their implications. These expressions are pregnant with meaning and strike a fatal blow against materialism. They refute any idea of self-sufficiency on man's part.

Materialistic culture overconfident about its resources

Materialistic culture stands out for its overconfidence about its means and resources. These materialistic states keep proclaiming their economic and sociological plans,[1] with precise goals. Without any regard for climatic changes and weather variations they fix their

---

[1] We are not opposed to drawing plans or to strive for increasing the produce on the basis of knowledge. What is meant is that the manifestations of power and abundance of knowledge should not turn us rebellious or make us forget the greatness and supremacy of Allah. For He is the Creator of all causes and effects.

yield and announce that they would attain self-sufficiency in production within a certain period, which would end all foreign assistance. However, Allah's will renders their plans null and void as they confront famine, flood, delayed monsoon or excessive rain which destroy harvest. Unexpected calamities befall and their plans are not materialized.

Trust in Allah's will

The expression *Inshā-Allah* (If Allah wills) should be used with reference to our routine jobs and travel plans and it should be borne in mind while drawing up grand plans which affect the whole nation. All striving for actualizing these plans, importance of means and resources and acting in conformity with the practice of the Prophet (peace be upon him) and this Companions should be subject to the realization that decision rests only with Allah:

Do not say about anything) "I will do this tomorrow." Rather say: "(I will do this tomorrow) if Allah wills so."

(18: 23-24)

The above verse is not addressed to that particular person; it is directed at every society, state, institution, organization and movement. They must act on it. It sums up the spirit of that Islamic society which is soaked in faith and rests on the pillar of belief in the unseen. This distinguishes it from the materialistic worldview. That believer warns his friend that the change in fortune and bestowal of prosperity and adversity are fully in Allah's hands. He exercises total control. A poor person may turn into a wealthy one overnight. Likewise, an affluent person may be reduced to a pauper. One should not be astonished over the sudden change in fortune:

If you consider me less in wealth and children, my Lord may give me something better than your garden. He may send some calamity from the heavens to your garden, which may reduce it to a plain waste field. Or the water of the garden may go underground and you may never get it.

(18: 39-41)

Exactly the same happened. A storm sent down by Allah, reduced the blossoming garden to a desolate field.

This awoke that arrogant person: His produce was destroyed. He was left rubbing his hands in sorrow over what he had spent on that garden. His garden had fallen down upon its foundations.

> He said: "I wish I had not taken any partner with my Lord." There was no group to help him against Allah. Nor could he be of any help to himself. All protection is from Allah, the true One. He is the best to reward and the best to give success.

(18: 42-44)

Polytheism committed by the owner of the two gardens

The owner of the two gardens was not an ordinary polytheist. Rather, it emerges from the Qur'anic style and context that he believed in Allah:

> I do not think there ever will be the Last Day. Even if I am returned to my Lord, I will get a better place.

(18: 36)

Yet he regretted what he committed:

> He said: "I wish I had not taken any partner with my Lord."

(18: 42)

It is evident that he had committed polytheism with reference to resources. He believed that he owed his prosperity and wealth to the apparent means and resources. Accordingly, he neglected Allah and denied His role and power.

Polytheism of our times

The present culture is afflicted with exactly the same kind of polytheism. It has idolised the specialists in various fields of physical and technological domains. Man today is totally dependent upon them. He thinks that these specialists decide his success or failure, honour or disgrace, and prosperity or adversity. Idolising material resources, forces of nature and over-dependence upon specialists and elevating them to Godhead are a new form of polytheism. It has been an addition to the pantheon of idolatry. We do have a record of idolatry and its adherents are still there in large numbers. This new type of polytheism is a rival of Faith and servitude to Allah. Surah Al-Kahf challenges this kind of polytheism and refutes it.

The Qur'an refers to the life in this world as that vegetation which is likely to wither away soon:

> Relate to them the parable of the life of this world. It is like rain which Allah sends down, which mixes with the produce of the earth. Then it becomes dry, which winds blow. Allah has power over everything.
>
> (18: 45)

At other places too, the Qur'an harps at the ephemeral nature of life in this world:

> The likeness of the life of this world is that is that of rain which God sent down from the sky. It causes the produce of the earth which provides food for men and animals. The earth too: its golden colour and was well adorned (with harvest) and the owners thought they had full control over their land. However, God's command came upon them by night or by day. And God reduced it to stubble as if it had not flourished a day ago. This is how God explains His signs for

those who reflect (on truth).

(10: 24)

The Qur'an discusses in the above passage the materialistic outlook on life, practised by the epicureans. It rejects their criteria on which they trust. It upholds the validity of the standards prescribed by Faith:

> Wealth and children are the glitter of this life. However, lasting things with your Lord are good actions. These will bring you reward and hope.

(18: 46)

This worldly life in the Qur'anic perspective

Let us reflect on the Qur'anic perspective on life. Our analysis should start with the relevant Qur'anic passages. Muslims are not very clear on this issue. Likewise, thinkers have divergent views on the topic.

Categorically and forcefully the Qur'an declares that this worldly life is brief and worthless as compared to the Next Life:

> The comfort of the life of this world is too little in comparison to the Next Life.

(9: 38)

Know well that the life of this world is play and sport, and show and boasting among you. You compete with one another in increasing wealth and children. The life of this world is like rain. Its produce delights farmers. However, it soon turns dry and yellow. Then it is reduced to pieces. There is terrible punishment in the Hereafter.

> There is, however, Allah's forgiveness and pleasure. The life of this world is no more than deception.

(57: 20)

According to the Qur'an, this life is an opportunity for reaping the benefits in the Hereafter:

Allah has made everything on earth pleasing in order to test as to who does good actions.

(18:7)

He has created death and life so that He may test as to who is best in action. He is Almighty, Most Forgiving.

(67: 2)

The Next Life is eternal and permanent:

The life of this world is only a sport and an amusement. The abode of the Hereafter is far better for the pious. Do you not understand?

(6: 32)

Whatever is given to you is for the life of this world and its glitter. However, what is with Allah is far better and long lasting. Do you not see?

(28:60)

The Qur'an denounces those who prefer the ephemeral, miserable life of this world to the Hereafter which is eternal, limitless and free from any imperfection or fear:

Those who do not expect to meet Allah, they are pleased and satisfied with the life of this world. They neglect Allah's signs.
The Hellfire is their abode. This is in return for what they used to do.

(10: 7-8)

He who is after the joys of the life of this world, Allah will pay the price of his actions in this world, without any decrease. However, there will be nothing for them in the Hereafter.

They will have there only the Hellfire. All of their actions will be reduced to nothing in the Hereafter. For their actions were worthless.

(11: 15-16)

At another place it asserts:

All that is in the heavens and on earth belongs to Allah. There is severe punishment and woe for the unbelievers. They prefer the life of this world to the Hereafter. They stop people from Allah's way and seek defects in it. They have gone too far into error.

(14:2-3)

They are only after the appearance of this worldly life while they neglect the Hereafter.

(30: 7)

(O Prophet), leave alone those who turn away from Allah's message. They want only the life of this world. This is the highest level of their knowledge. Your Lord knows best who are away from His path and those who are guided.

(54: 29-30)

These unbelievers love (the life of) this world, neglecting the hard Day ahead of them.

(76: 27)

He who crossed the limits, and preferred the life of this world, Hell will be his home.

(79: 37-39)

The Qur'an praises those who work for both the worlds while placing premium on the Hereafter, as they recognize its importance and value:

Some people pray) "O our Lord, give us good in this world."
Such will have no share in the Hereafter. Some people pray)
"O our lord, give us good in this world and good in the Next
Life, and save us from the Hellfire."

(2: 200-201)

Prophet Musa (peace be upon him) affirms the same truth:

"Grant us good in this world and in the Hereafter. We
have turned to You."

(7:156)

While extolling Prophet Ibrahim (peace be upon him) the Qur'an
asserts:

"Allah gave him good in this life. In the Next Life he will be
among the pious."

(16:122)

Distinction between the Scriptures and Materialistic philosophical thought patterns:

There is a world of difference in the approaches of the religions
based on the Scriptures and Prophetic teachings and the
materialistic, philosophical thought patterns and their worldview.
For the latter, this life is all in all. Their only noble objective is to make
this life all the more comfortable and attractive.

The Qur'anic worldview on this worldly life is reflected clearly in
Prophet Muhammad's sayings. Often did he remark: "O Allah, the
only life is the Next Life."[2] His supplication was: "O Allah, provide
the family of Muhammad with only that much sustenance which is
sufficient for them."[3] Mastur ibn Shaddad reports the Prophet
(peace be upon him) remarking: "By Allah, this world in comparison

---

[2] *Sahih Bukhāri*, "Kitab Al-Riqaq."
[3] *Sahih Muslim*, "Kitab Al-Zuhd."

of the Hereafter is as if one dips his finger in an ocean and then see how much water it can draw."[4] The Prophet's pious, blessed life was illustrative of the same belief system and psyche.

Ibn Mas'ud recounts: "The Prophet (peace be upon him) was reclining on a mat and its marks were visible on his body. I said: "O Messenger of Allah, you should have asked us to spread a sheet over the mat." Upon this he said: "I have nothing to do with this world. I am like a rider in this world who takes rest for a while under the shade of a tree and then moves on his way."[5]

Another report on the authority of 'Umar ibn Khattab reads as follows: I called on the Prophet (peace be upon him) while he was reclining on a coarse mat. This mat had no sheet or mattress. One could see the imprint of the mat on his body. He was sitting, reclining against a leather pillow, stuffed with straw. I greeted him. As I looked around, by Allah, it had nothing which could draw anyone's attention. He had only three leather pieces. I requested him: "Please pray to Allah for the prosperity of the Muslim community."

The Persians and Romans have plenty of bounties, though they do not worship Allah." Upon hearing all this, Prophet Muhammad (peace be upon him) rose, saying: "O Ibn Khattab, even you think like this! They are the ones who have been recompensed for the bounties in this world."[6]

Character of those trained by the Prophet (peace be upon him)

The Prophet's Companions imbibed in full the Prophet's training. They were concerned all the time about the Hereafter. Rather, this concern permeated every fibre of their body. They did not neglect it even for a moment. Nor were they willing to accept anything in exchange for it. For appreciating better the spirit enveloping the heart and mind of these Companions, a study of the

---

[4] *Sahih Muslim,* "Kitab Al-Zuhd."

[5] Ahmad, Tirmidhi and Ibn Majah

[6] *Sahih Bukhāri,* "Kitab Al-Nikah."

life and attributes of 'Ali ibn Abi Talib is sufficient. His is the model of someone trained by the Prophet (peace be upon him), rather someone brought up under his affectionate care and guidance.

Abu Salih reports: "Mu'awiyah ibn Abu Sufyan requested Zarrar ibn Zamrah to tell him something about the character and conduct of 'Ali. He first excused himself. However, at the insistence of Mu'awiyah he told: "By Allah, he was a far-sighted, strong and energetic person. He minced no words in conveying what he intended. He adjudged cases justly. Knowledge was his main strength and as a result, wisdom permeated his sayings. He was indifferent to the charms of this life and felt at home in the darkness of night. By Allah, he used to cry much and felt concerned about his self development. His dress was coarse and his food was ordinary and bland. He mixed with us fully and behaved like one of us. He responded quickly to our queries, greeted us as we arrived and was the first to greet and welcome us. Whenever we invited, he joined us. Notwithstanding his affection and Kindness we held him in awe and could not talk to him properly. When he smiled, there flashed a string of pearls. He honoured the weak and the poor. No one, however influential, could expect his decision unduly favouring him. Nor was any weak person in doubt about his integrity. While taking Allah as the witness let me tell you that I saw him at special hours in the darkness of night, with the stars about to set. I found him standing at his prayer mat, holding his beard and appeared so restless as if he had been bitten by a snake. He cried profusely as a bereaved person. I can recall what he said then: "O world, do you want to obstruct or tempt me? Woe to you! You may deceive others. I have already abandoned you and will not be attracted by you any longer. This life is too brief and dangerous. I have little for the Next Life. It is a long, terrible way to the Next Life."[7]

Another example is the following address by a Companion at a major Muslim town:

Khalid ibn 'Umayr Al-Adawiy reports: "Utbah ibn Ghazwan, chief

---

[7] Ibn Jawzi, *Sifwat al-Sifwah*

of Basrah, delivered his address. After praising and glorifying Allah he said: "Certainly this world is about to end. It has been swiftly completing its term. Little time is now left. All of you are to be transferred from here to an eternal abode. You should better go there, with some good deeds to your credit. For we have been informed that a stone thrown into Hell will take seventy years to reach its bottom. And Hell is to be filled with human beings. Are you astonished over this? And we have also been informed that the distance of threshold of the gate of Paradise takes forty years to cover. There will be a day when Paradise will be full of human beings. We spent seven consecutive days while subsisting on leaves of trees. Our mouths were hurt, taking this unpalatable food. I got hold of a cloth sheet which I tore into two, and gave one part of to Sa'id ibn Malik and I wore the other. Now each one of us is a ruler of a major town. I seek Allah's refuge against self-aggrandizement while I may be worthless in the eyes of Allah."[8]

Modern mindset and its poor understanding of the doctrine of the Hereafter

Those minds and movements that have not fully grasped Faith and who were not directly trained by the Prophet (peace be upon him) have not followed this doctrine, concern or interest. Nor do they want to learn more about it. They are uncertain about it. They do not seem very keen on discussing it, as a true disciple of the Prophet (peace be upon him) should be. They want to escape from it, arguing that the above discourse was for a particular time and context. These directives were needed at a certain point of time. However, it is an open secret that the concern for the Hereafter permeates the Qur'an and Prophet Muhammad's *sirah*. It represents the true Islamic spirit and mindset which was nurtured under the Prophet's care. The Qur'an and *sirah* mould the mind along the same lines of a generation, which is free from external influence and is brought up in purely Islamic ethos. Such Islamically trained people avoid worldliness, are content, and feel deeply concerned about the Next

---

[8] *Sahih Muslim*, "Kitab Al-Zuhd."

Life and those deeds which may benefit them there. They are very particular about appearing before Allah, prefer the Next Life to the present. They love to die in the state of belief and welcome death in the cause of Allah. These believers follow this motto of the Prophet's Companions and early Muslims: "Tomorrow we will meet our friends and beloved ones, Prophet Muhammad (peace be upon him) and his Companions."[9]

The Prophet's call and its difference with reform movements

Some groups and movements expound well the belief in the Hereafter and bring out its rationale, benefits and its healthy impact on life cogently. Also, these discuss its importance in the moral system. However, any discerning person may realize that they use the doctrine of the Hereafter only as a moral imperative and as the means and cause for reform. For, without this doctrine a better, pious society cannot be constructed. This approach is laudable on some counts. However, it differs from the way of Prophets, their methodology and character and the lifestyle of their votaries. The Prophets' way consists in faith, intuition, cognitive faculty, and a keen desire. This belief system grips the whole range of human emotions. The latter may take into consideration only its legal form. When the people belonging to the former category mention the Hereafter, they relish it with ecstasy and natural feelings. They present this doctrine with fervour and conviction. The latter group speaks of it only as a social and moral necessity for reform and moral code. There is a world of difference in the above two approaches, of which the details cannot be discussed in this work owing to the constraints of space.

The biggest motivating factor and source of strength for moving forward

The conviction in the Hereafter, preference to it over this world,

---

[9] This is the saying of Bilal ibn Rabah Al-Habshi (*Ihyā al- 'ulum* on the authority of Ibn Abi Al-Dunya).

and disregard for the charms and adornments of this world did not impel the Prophet's Companion to neglect their role as the leader of the world and mentor of mankind. Under its influence they did not renounce life. Nor did they turn away from economic pursuits. They did not relinquish their struggle for truth. Their faith saved them against the feelings of defeatism, as was witnessed in later centuries. Rather, it was the source of strength, initiative and crusade against evil. It was the means for their bravery, victory and dynamism. Those who were not worldly, and were devoted to the Hereafter and very keen about appearing before Allah and sacrificing their lives in His cause turned out to be the most resilient, brave and heroic as they contributed immensely to the cause of truth, *Jihād*, self sacrifice and Islamic conquests.

This doctrine naturally prompts its believers to disregard worldly life, exercise self-restraint with regard to desire and display manliness and truthfulness. Needless to add, the same doctrine was a driving force behind the Islamic conquests and progress and the phenomenal spread of Islam.

Nothing in common between the belief in the Hereafter and Monasticism

The Qur'anic stance on the belief in the Hereafter and disregard for this worldly life has nothing in common with that detestable monasticism which is condemned by the Qur'an. This weakness arose in the Muslim world as the impact of Islamic teachings turned weaker and non-Islamic forces and philosophical thought, including Christianity, Buddhism, Brahmanism and Neo-Platonism had greater influence on Muslims.

The Islamic stance does not deny what is due in the life and does not reject its true worth. Yet it prefers the Hereafter and for its sake believers control, rather sacrifice their desires and focus on securing Allah's pleasure. As Muslims did not adhere to this doctrine, they became weaker. The present day Muslim generations are under the sway of base desires. Hence the above belief must be reinvigorated and promoted among Muslims. This imbalance will not be removed and Muslims will not fulfil the requisites of faith unless they lead life in accordance with the Qur'an. This is something deeply resented by the materialists. For they are given to materialism, worship of life, obsessed with desires and are under the control of their base self. Their only objective is prosperity in this world, happiness and comfort. They do not want anything beyond this. They are not willing to strike any deal.

Surah Al-Kahf strikes forcefully at the roots of this materialistic outlook on life, and its votaries. It projects that worldview which is sound and true, no matter whether people like it or not.

Chapter 3

STORY OF PROPHET MUSA AND KHIDR

The encounter between Prophet Musa (peace be upon him) and Khidr (peace be upon him)

Let us now turn to the story of Prophet Musa (peace be upon him) and Khidr (peace be upon him) which is related to this life and this world inhabited by all of us. It proves conclusively that there is much in this world which is unknown, of which even well-informed scholars are unaware. Man's ignorance exceeds his knowledge, Man infers things through his observation and perception and hence he often errs and stumbles. Were the secrets of life to come to man's knowledge, his outlook will change greatly and he will have to alter his decisions. We learn from this story that one's opinion or perception is not unreliable. It is not possible to fathom the secrets of this universe.

Therefore, it is not proper to insist on one's decision. Life is too ambivalent and mysterious, comprising several layers. Its outward appearance and innermost reality are poles apart. Life abounds in riddles which man, despite his sharp mind, has not been able to resolve. All knowledge is still insufficient to solve these mysteries. Our daily life is marred by blunders, hasty rulings, emotional responses and superficial views. Were this vast universe to be managed by man with total power and freedom, there will be chaos and corruption. Future generations will also be affected by this disaster. What accounts for it is that man's vision is too narrow and limited. He is hasty and impatient by nature.

For unraveling the above truth and for affirming the belief in the unseen, which is at the core of all religions, Allah selected an outstanding personality of the day who was endowed with knowledge, goodness and piety. It was Prophet Musa (peace be upon him), a leading Prophet. Once while addressing the children of Isra'il, he was asked as to who is the most knowledgeable person, he named himself. Allah did not like his reply. For he had not attributed his knowledge to Allah and asserted his own knowledge. Allah informed him of Khidr, based at the convergence of the two seas, who possessed more knowledge than him.[1]

Unusual conditions

Musa (peace be upon him) accompanied someone on a journey. Allah had granted that person His special mercy and knowledge. There was a clash of opinions between the two on three occasions.

Khidr boards a boat and its owner does not charge even any money from him yet he damages that boat. Musa (peace be upon him) records his dissent and on the basis of his knowledge and understanding he questions this decision.

Then Khidr kills an innocent youth who had not wronged him. Likewise, he repairs a wall which was about to collapse in a town, though its residents had refused to host him. All these three actions of Khidr were intriguing and astonished Musa (peace be upon him), prompting him to question him. For the boat, which was crucial to their voyage, was not to be damaged, especially in view of the favour done by its owner. The boat owner should have been thanked, rather than be treated so harshly. Similarly, that youth deserved love and affection. He stood in need of care and upbringing.

The people of the town were too rude. They had refused any hospitality and hence in these three instances what Khidr did was not expected of him in usual circumstances. His actions appeared illogical. Prophet Musa (peace be upon him) being a Messenger of Allah was a sensitive soul and could not put up with anything wrong. He could not be a silent spectator to these strange actions. While forgetting his promise, he expresses his bewilderment and opposition, saying:

---

[1] *Sahih Al-Bukhāri,* "Kitab Al-Tafsir"

They travelled together and met a boy. He killed him. Moses said: "You killed an innocent person, who had not killed anyone. You have done something dreadful."

(18: 74)

Facts stranger than fiction

Khidr deferred his reply to Musa's questions and persisted calmly in his business. When the journey was over, he explained the rationale behind his actions. He pointed to the reality which was incomprehensible to Prophet Musa (peace be upon him). On reading this story in the Qur'an, one readily recognises that Khidr was in the right. On all three occasions he acted tactfully. He did not mix up anything good with evil. By damaging the boat he did a favour, as it helped its poor owner retain his boat. For at that time the king was acquiring all working boats. Khidr repaid the favour of boarding the boat without any charge by protecting it against the king's unjust acquisition of boats.

Khidr also did a favour to the parents of that boy. For he was likely to be a serious trial for them. Had he survived, he could commit rebellion and unbelief.

Therefore, Khidr decided that the trouble should be better nipped in the bud. Their son could be replaced whereas faith is irreplaceable:

As to the boy, his parents were believers. I feared that he will hurt them with his rebellion and unbelief. I desired that their Lord should give his parents another son in his place, better in conduct and affection.

(18: 80-81)

Khidr repaired the wall in that it belonged to two orphan boys and beneath it lay their treasure. Had it collapsed, the treasure could be looted while its heirs, the young orphans would have got nothing. A good deed benefits one even after his death. Allah did not want to deprive the children of that pious person's treasure. He did not leave that person's children in a helpless condition:

Their Lord accepted their prayer, saying: "I do not lay to waste the action of any of you, male or female."

(3: 195)

Allah does not let the reward of pious persons to go to waste.

(12: 90)

Actions, like seeds, have their good or evil results: "As for the wall, it belonged to two orphans in the town. A treasure belonging to them was under it. Their father was a pious person. So your Lord decided that when they come of age, they may take out their treasure as mercy from your Lord. So I did not do anything of my own. This is the truth of the things about which you could not have patience."

(18: 82)

Human knowledge cannot attain perfection

The truth behind events is very strange in view of the stark contrast between the outward and the inward. So is life, full of complexity. The riddles of life are unfathomable. Yet man audaciously claims that he has found out everything, including its underlying cause. It appears *prima facie* that Khidr was unaware of truth. His actions lacked balance. Eventually, however, he proved to be true. His opinion was sane and sensible. Life is full of marvels. And one realizes that knowledge is limitless and it is beyond man to master it:

Allah is All Knowing, far above all those who have some knowledge.

70

(12: 76)

A challenge to the materialistic outlook

This story, in its contents and messages, challenges that materialist philosophy which holds a superficial, shallow view of life and its false claim of possessing all knowledge. It believes only in tangible entities and appearances. It demands that man be entrusted with the job of managing this world, including legislation. For man's knowledge, reason, study and research are perfect, with access to the depths of knowledge and truth.

This has been at the core of all materialistic philosophical thought. Modern culture shares the same view. Surah Al- Kahf in general, and the story of Prophet Musa (peace be upon him) and Khidr in particular bust this myth. Significantly, this story concludes with this Qur'anic verse:

> This is the truth of the things about which you could not have patience.

(18: 82)

Haste, rejection and error are innate in the human- nature. Truth[2] ultimately prevails and establishes its supremacy.

The fourth story in this Surah is of a person who was blessed with superior power, natural resources and control over the forces created for man. He deployed all the resources against corrupt, rebellious and tyrannical rulers for the objectives of human prosperity, serving mankind and constructing a pious society.

---

[2] Ibn Taimiyyah, *Tafsir Surah Al-Ikhlās.*

Chapter 4

THE STORY OF DHŪ L-QARNAYN

Dhū l-Qarnayn and the construction of the iron barrier

There is some divergence of opinion on the identity of Dhū l‑Qarnayn. The majority view is that the allusion is to Alexandar of Macedonia, a view shared and upheld by Imam Razi. Most of the Islamic scholars endorse this view. However, there is not much substance in this hypothesis. For Alexandar is bereft of the traits mentioned by the Qur'an in the context of Dhū l‑Qarnayn and kindness towards the conquered people and the construction of the barrier.

This view does not take into account the profile and military expeditions of Alexander. Some scholars of the day[1] identify him

---

[1] This is the view put forth in some detail by Mawlana Abul Kalam Azad in volume 2 of the *Tarjumān al-Qur'ān* wherein he has adduced numerous references from historical treatises and Jewish religious records in support of his thesis. A summary of it is given here. A remarkable personality came to the fore in a dramatic manner in 559BC and soon attracted the attention of the whole world. Persia was then divided into two Kingdoms) the southern part was known as Persia and the north-western portion was called Media (Araba called it Mahat). Cyrus welded the Persian tribes into a single nation by defeating Astyages of Media at Pasargadae. Thereafter began the conquests of Cyrus, which were marked not by sanguine battles and cruelties but by humanity and mindfulness to the vanquished inhabitants and honour to the defeated monarchs. Within 12 years all the lands from Black Sea to Bactria had been reduced to the position of Persian dependencies. In the spring of 546 B.C. Croesus of Lydia attacked Persia, Cyrus flung himself upon him, beat him at Pteria in Cappadocia and pursued him to Lydia, the North-Western part of Asia Minor, which was then the centre of Hellenistic civilization in Asia. A second victory followed on the banks of Pactolus: by the autumn of 546 B.C. Sardis had already fallen, and the Persian forces advanced to the bounds of Mediterranean. During the next few years, the Greek littoral towns were reduced. In 539 B.C. Nabonidus was defeated and Babylon occupied, which, with the Chaldean empire, Syria and Palestine also became Persian. When Cyrus would have advanced beyond Sardis he must have turned back from the coast of Aegean Sea, near Smyrna. Here he would have seen the sea taking the shape of a lake and the sun setting in the murky

with Cyrus. In our opinion, Sayyid Qutb's opinion is very apt. In his *Tafsir fi Zilāl al-Qur'ān* he remarks:

The Qur'an does not specify the identity or the time and place of Dhū l-Qarnayn.

This is a style of narration peculiar to the stories mentioned in the Qur'an, for its aim is not to historicize the events but to draw out the moral and lesson of the story. The purpose can very often be achieved without determining the location and chronology of the events mentioned in the Qur'an.

Our recorded history does mention an emperor by the name of Alexander Dhū l-Qarnayn but it is certain that he was not the personality meant by the Qur'an. Alexander the great was a polytheist and   an idol worshipper while the sovereign mentioned in the Qur'an was a man of Allah, a Unitarian, having faith in the Day of Judgment, Resurrection, etc.

In his book entitled *Al-Āthār-ul Baqiyah an- al-Qurron il-Khaliyah* Abu Rayhan al-Bairuni writes that Dhū l-Qarnayn spoken of in the

---

water: "he found it setting in a muddy spring," as the Qur'an puts it. (18:87) In his eastward expedition, Cyrus conquered the lands up to Makran and Balkh. In this religion he subdued the uncivilized nomadic tribes, which have also been referred to in the Qur'an: "He found it (sun) raising on a people for whom We had appointed no shelter therefrom" (18:91). After reducing Babylon, Cyrus rescued the Jews from the tyranny of Nabonidus, as predicted in the Jewish Scriptures. He permitted the Jews in Babylon to return and rebuild Jerusalem. The last campaign of Cyrus was in the direction of the lands despoiled by the people called Gog and Magog. Cyrus advanced towards Caucasus, leaving Caspian Sea to his right, where he came across a mountain pass between two steep hills rising live walls. Here is constructed the iron rampart to check the ingress of Gog and Magog. Cyrus met his end in 529B.C. A marble statue with two horns on his head, signifying the unified kingdoms of Persia and Media, was recovered from the ruins of Pasargadae in 1938. The unification of these two kingdoms gave Cyrus the title of   Dhu Al-Qarnayn. Cyrus has been rightly praised by most of the modern historians for his conquests as well as for his just and mild treatment of the conquered people (For further details see *Universal History of the World*, vol. II, by J. A. Hammerton).

Qur'an belonged to Hymar, as the name itself indicates. The kings of Hymar had the prefix *Dhū* as an essential part of their names as, e.g. Dhū-Nuwas, Dhū-Yazan. The proper name of Dhū l-Qarnayn was Abu Bakr Ibn Afriqash. He subdued all the lands on the coast of Mediterranean Sea, including Tunis and Morocco, and founded a city called *Afriqiah* which gave its name to the entire continent. He was called by the name of Dhū l-Qarnayn, as he was believed to have reached the lands of the rising and setting sun.

This view might be correct but we have no means to verify it. The extant records of history hardly contain anything about him, and the description of his character and conquests given in the Qur'an is too general like that of the peoples of Nuh, Hud, Salih, etc. Actually, the records preserved by our history constitute only a fraction of our life- story on this earth. We have no record of the events that took place before history began to list them. Its verdict is thus not at all reliable.

If only the Old Testament could have preserved in its pristine purity without interpolations and additions, it could have served as a valuable source of history. But, unfortunately, numerous legends have been introduced and interwoven with the revelation contained in this Scripture with the result that historical events mentioned in it cannot be relied upon.

The Qur'an being free from all additions, alterations and mutilations can, undoubtedly, be a trustworthy source of the events narrated by it, but its version cannot obviously be verified from historical records. This is because of two reasons; first, history does not account for innumerable happenings; and, secondly, the Qur'an unfolds some of those events of the olden times which have not been recorded at all.

There is another reason too. Recorded history, even if it contains the details of any particular happening, is, after all, a human endeavour always likely to commit mistakes or misrepresent the event in question. With all the facilities of communication, means of transmitting news and techniques of their verification in the modern times, we sometimes come across different versions of one and the same story. The same event is not un-often interpreted differently, viewed from different angles and widely differing conclusions are drawn there from. This is, in truth, the basic material which serves as the source of history: it is, however, an entirely different matter that we have devised elaborate norms for post-scrutiny and verification of the authenticity of the material thus collected.

Therefore, it is against the accepted principles of literary criticism as well as Qur'anic exegesis to seek historical evidence for the verification of events related by the Qur'an. Moreover, this procedure is also not in accord with the conviction which claims to profess the Qur'an as eternal, unchangeable word of Allah. Absolute reliance cannot, obviously, be placed on the data thus collected by history either by one having faith in the revelatory nature of the Qur'an or by an impartial literary critic. Historical data is, at best, no more than a collection of our impressions, estimates and ideas about the past happenings.

The Prophet had been asked about Dhū l-Qarnayn. Thereupon Allah revealed certain salient characteristics of the monarch known by that name. Now, the Qur'an being the only source of knowledge about him, the verification of its historicity or otherwise is beyond our means. The commentaries on the Qur'an present differing views in the matter and, therefore, reliance cannot be placed on them. If any particular view is endorsed by any commentator, he ought to be extremely cautious for numerous traditions of yore and Israelite legends have found their way into some of the old commentaries.[2]

A righteous and reformist king

We may not accurately identify the personality referred to as Dhū l-Qarnayn in the Qur'an. History does not help us much in this regard, for it was documented at a later date.

This lack of accuracy is not a serious matter for a student of the Qur'an. For the Qur'an has provided an extensive account of his traits. Allah had blessed him with power, means, resources, high spirit,

---

[2] Sayyid Qutb, *Fi Zilāl al-Qur'ān.* 6: 8-10.

ambition and large-heartedness:

> Allah had granted him power on earth. He had given him all
> kinds of things. He set out one way (westwards).
>
> (18: 84-85)

The range of his conquests was very wide, from one corner of the east to the other of the west, as is specified in the Qur'an. In all of his conquests, however, he behaved as a righteous, reformist king who stood for truth, supported the weak and was a scourge against the rebels and wrongdoers. His mission, according to the Qur'an, was:

> He said: "I will punish him who does wrong. He will be then
> returned to his Lord Who will punish him hard. As for him who
> believes and does good, there is an excellent reward for him. I
> will treat him kindly."
>
> (18:87-88)

One need not emphasize the features of piety, truthfulness, balance, moral excellence and good character and conduct in the above statement.

During this phase of his conquests, he passed by a people who were settled between mountains, and were vulnerable to attacks by a barbaric people on the other side of mountains. The Qur'an and other Scriptures speak of the latter as Gog (*Yājuj*) and Magog (*Mājuj*).[3]

---

[3] We fully share Qutb's view on this issue. In his words, "we cannot specify the exact location of where Dhu Al-Qarnayn had passed between the two passes. Nor can we say anything with certainly about these two passes. What we learn from the primary Islamic sources is that he reached a valley which was located between the two passes, and which was inhabited by a weak, backward community that hardly understood anything." (Al-Kahf 18:93). As to the following issues, the identity and ethnicity of *Yājuj* and *Mājuj*, their era, the date of their appearance when they will demolish the wall, it calls for a long discussion. It is covered in the works on *tafsir* and *ahādith*, which deal with the signs and wars in a period close to the Last Day. It is not easy to reach any definite conclusion on these issues. Those interested in the topic should study the writings of both classical and recent writers, and this material is not too bulky. However, the study of the *ahādith* related to the period close to the Last Day awaits a spirited scholar well versed in religious studies and history who

These people were afflicted with civil war and internecine feuds:

On that Day Allah will release them like waves against one another.

(18: 99)

When they came across Dhū l- Qarnayn, they realised that it was a God-sent opportunity for them, as Allah had introduced them to a powerful, pious king. They requested him to secure their defence against their barbaric neighbours who were given to corruption and wrongdoing. They pleaded with him to erect a wall or barrier between the two while deploying his vast resources and army. That would bar *Yājuj* (Gog) and *Mājuj* (Magog) from attacking them frequently.

They offered to contribute financially to this project.

The pious Dhū l-Qarnayn gracefully accepted their request and promised to build that barrier. However, he did not accept their offer of financial contribution, unlike the greedy kings who are after money. He, nonetheless, asked them to help his army with manpower and the local supply of iron:

He replied: "What my Lord has given me is enough. You only assist me with labour. I will make a strong wall between you and them. Bring me blocks of iron."

(18: 95-96)

All of them cooperated in the construction of this valuable and welcome barrier. The righteous king applied his expertise and the locals their manpower and raw material such as iron to this project:

---

may undertake painstaking, thorough study of the subject. He should be sincere and devout. For the topic is important and broad, calling for much caution and care.

Bring me blocks of iron. As he filled up the space between the two mountains, he asked them to (light fire) and blow it. When he made the wall red like fire, he told them: "Bring me molten fire which I will pour on it."

(18: 96)

As this wall was erected, it provided safety against those living outside the mountains:

So they (*Yājuj* and *Mājuj*) could not climb it. Nor could they dig through it.

(18: 97)

Insights of a sagacious believer

On this occasion, this grand king who had conquered many countries, did not make any boastful comment. Nor was he afflicted with any arrogance or negligence. He was a devout person. He did not brag that "he possessed things because of the knowledge given to him" (28:70).[4] Rather, he ascribed everything to Allah. He did not consider the construction of that wall as his ever-lasting achievement. As an insightful, sagacious Muslim believing in the Hereafter and aware of man's weakness and vicissitudes of times, he said only this much:

Dhū l-Qarnayn said: "This is mercy from my Lord. When it is time for my Lord's promise to come true, He will level it. My Lord's promise is true."

(18: 98)

Dhū l-Qarnayn was powerful and well informed and had conquered material resources and exercised control over the means and resources. His range of military conquests was very wide. However, even at the height of his power and rule he never forgot his Lord and surrendered himself to Allah. For he was concerned with the

---

[4] "All this has been given to me because of a certain knowledge that I have." (28:78).

Hereafter and was in constant fear of it. He admits his humanness and bestows kindness and mercy on humanity, especially the weak. He stands for truth and devotes all his energy, talents and resources to serving humanity, constructing a pious society, upholding the Word of Allah in order to draw people from darkness into light. His aim is to guide people to serving Allah by abandoning materialism. The same character was displayed in their respective eras by Prophet Sulayman (peace be upon him), son of Prophet Dawud (peace be upon him), the rightly guided Caliphs and leading Islamic scholars.

Chapter 5

FALLACY OF MATERIALISM

Rebellion against the Creator of the universe is innate in the Western culture. One of the tragedies in history is the evolution of the Western culture at a time when rebellion against religion and rejection of the belief in the unseen had become fairly common. The Westerners were opposed to the clergy that had abused religion for gratifying their base desires, egotism and vested interests. Their evil character, bigotry, opposition to progress and obstructions against reason and knowledge had earned public ire.[1] As a result of this, the evolution of culture and industry and the new way of life were on patently materialistic basis. Society and individuals snapped their ties with their Lord, the Creator and Master of the universe. All this flowed from a chain of cause and effect, temperament, outlook on life, peculiar circumstances and the typical European lifestyle. This new culture rested on the pillars of atheism and moral degeneration. The West has touched the new heights of industrial progress, and accumulation of knowledge. Distance has lost its meaning and man has experimented with the astronomical space. Eventually man has landed on the moon. Man has made many advancements in physics and astronomy.

As a result of this excessive materialism, control over natural forces and the universe and unbelief have joined hands and this is an outstanding feature of Western civilization. We are not aware of any other culture or civilization that was so hostile to religion and morals notwithstanding its vast material resources. It is opposed to the Creator of the universe and His law, and is given to materialism, gratifying the base self and claims lordship.

---

[1] See Nadwi, *Rise and Fall of Muslim*, 1-48.

Culmination of the Materialistic culture

As already discussed, the Western civilization has evolved in a way that despite its control over material resources it denies Allah. Its proponents believe in only their own power.

They are driven by selfish motives. Its main centres namely, the USA, Europe and Russia, publicly or implicitly oppose the truths related to the unseen, spirituality, morals and celestial order. The day is not very far when this civilization will reach the highest point of industrial and material progress and its massive manifestation will appear which is called *Dajjāl* in the Prophetic parlance. It will mark the height of material of and industrial progress on the one hand, and unbelief, materialism, atheism, worship of the forces of nature and servitude to those controlling these, on the other. It would be the most serious trial and mischief for humanity and the culmination of the materialistic culture that originated from Europe a few centuries ago.

Signs of *Dajjāl*: Unbelief, corruption and disaster

We have depicted above the facets of the industrial, mechanistic and materialistic culture, which is about to reach its culmination point. It would be eventually led by *Dajjāl*. Prophet Muhammad (peace be upon him) has condemned *Dajjāl* and warned against the mischief erected by it. This is a significant point. Otherwise, material resources and power were possessed by Prophet Sulayman (peace be upon him) and Dhū l-Qarnayn in abundance. The Qur'an speaks of their power and control over means and resources. Let us consider what distinguishes *Dajjāl* from them. For the Qur'an praises the powerful, righteous king:

Allah granted Solomon to David. He was an excellent servant of Allah. He turned much to Allah.

(38:30)

Prophet Muhammad (peace be upon him) has eloquently warned the Muslim community against *Dajjal* and explained at length the traits of *Dajjal.*

The distinguishing mark is that Prophet Sulayman (peace be upon him), Dhū l-Qarnayn and the early Islamic role models combined in them the following traits: superior power, a vast range of conquests, exceptional wisdom and insights, noble objectives, a call to turn to Allah and using the knowledge, wisdom, energy and resources for the welfare of fellow human beings, and for ensuring fairness and justice. Allah extols them thus:

> Were Allah to give them authority on earth, they will regularly offer Prayer, pay *zakāh* (charity), command good and forbid evil. With Allah is the end of all matters.

(22: 41)

> Allah has made the abode of the Hereafter exclusive for those who do not seek glory on earth and do not cause any mischief. The pious will have the best end.

(28: 83)

In contrast, according to the Prophet (peace be upon him), unbelief is the main feature of *Dajjal.* Here unbelief is used in a very bread sense. In the following authentic *hadith*, it is stated: "Unbelief will be writ large between his eyes and it will be comprehensible to every believer, both literate and illiterate."[2]

Impact of *Dajjal* on life and society

It emerges from the *ahādith* that *Dajjal* will be exceptionally active, shrewd and mobile, always engaged in the rebellion against religions and morals. The Prophet (peace be upon him) is on record,

---

[2] *Sahih Bukhāri*

saying: "By Allah, one will approach *Dajjāl*, taking him as a believer and will become his follower. Then *Dajjāl* will sow doubts into his heart."[3]

Dajjāl's call be will so widespread that no family will be safe against it, including females. All will be spellbound by him. The head of the family will be unable to exercise any control over his family members, wife, women and daughters. All will have unbridled freedom. It is stated in *hadith*: "*Dajjāl* will settle down in a barren piece of land known as Marraqanat. Women, while abandoning their family, will join them. One will be forced into imprisoning his own mother, daughter, sister and aunt so that they do not join *Dajjāl*."[4] The degeneration in society will reach its nadir, as indicated in this *hadith:* "Only the evil ones will be there, all over the place. They will be shallow like birds and behave like beasts as they will not have any regard for good or evil."[5]

The above presents a graphic picture of the materialistic culture of unbelief and its high point. It identifies its sites.

The above is reflective of the Prophet's miracle and his eloquent utterances, of which the wonders will never cease. It will remain fresh and meaningful forever. Undoubtedly the present culture is marred by shallowness. Like birds man soars high and flies in the sky, and has conquered space. Modern man is as swift as a bird in his place. At the same time, he is infested with beastly features, blood thirstiness and misanthropy. He feels no qualms of conscience in ethnic cleansing. People destroy ripe crops, gardens and orchards at a scale unprecedented in history. People have been behaving thus while they are blessed with abundant luxury, comfort, provisions and adornment. These resources were not aplenty earlier. According to the *hadith*, "It will be at a time when they will have abundant provisions and all the means for comfort and luxury."[6]

---

[3] *Abu Dāwud.*
[4] *Tabarāni* on the authority of Ibn 'Amr.
[5] *Sahih Muslim* (Narrated by 'Abdullah ibn 'Amr ibn al-As).
[6] *Sahih Muslim* (Narrated by 'Abdullah ibn 'Umar).

Self-delusion

As already indicated, this culture denies everything other than this material world and this worldly life. They waste their talent and energy on entertainment, charms of this life and fun. The concluding verses of Surah Al-Kahf eloquently warn against this. These address specifically the proponents of the Materialistic culture and their disciples in the Muslim world and portray them dexterously.

These verses expose the evil character and conduct of the upholders of the materialistic culture:

> When they are told not to make mischief on earth, they say: "We want only to set things right."

> (2: 11)

The above portrait applies to a great extent to the Jews who have neglected the Hereafter, despite many lessons and warnings to them. It condemns their activities at the global scale which have played an important role in the developments in industry, science, politics, governance and intellect. They have abused their exceptional mental prowess only for causing destruction, chaos and anarchy and for vindicating their racial supremacy i.e. of the Israelites as the chosen people of Allah:

> Say: "Should I tell you of those whose actions lead to their loss? Those whose all efforts are wasted for the life of this world. They, however, imagine that they are doing something good. Those who reject the signs of their Lord and their appearing before Him, all of their actions go to waste. Allah will not give any credit to them on the Day of Judgment."

> (18: 103-105)

Myopic human knowledge and understanding

The Qur'an strikes at the limited view of the universe and narrow human knowledge, though man claims to possess the knowledge of the universe. He thinks that the heavens and the earth, all the creatures and entities, stars and planets, land and sea and the vast space are under his control. He wants to appropriate for himself all that belongs to the divine knowledge. He boasts about his knowledge of the universe. However, in truth, man's knowledge is no more than a single drop of a vast ocean or a speck of dust of a big desert. This self-aggrandizement, boastfulness, overconfidence about his body of knowledge, denial of all else, arrogance, and self-centeredness betray his limited understanding and myopic vision. This mindset lies at the core of the Materialistic thought.

This human psyche is perverted and the same prompts him to perpetrate wrongs and rise in revolt, and even claim divinity for himself. It impels him to persecute those who are blessed with far-sightedness and discernment by Allah, as we learn from the story of the people of the Cave. In the other story of the owner of the two gardens we see the following despicable traits of the perverted human mind: belief in only here and now, love of this temporary, mirage- like life, belief in the everlasting nature of the comforts of the present life and disdain for those who have limited material resources. In the story of Prophet Musa (peace be upon him) and Khidr we see again the same mindset expressing astonishment over its own notions of right and wrong or logical thinking.

At times, this limited vision mixes up things, as for example, Dhū l- Qarnayn thought that the sun was about to set in dark waters:

> He reached the limits of the place where the sun sets. He saw there the sun setting in dark waters.

(18:86)

Likewise, the queen of Saba had an optic illusion as she entered the palace made of glass. She mistook crystal for the flowing water and bared her ankles:

> She was told to enter the palace. When she saw it, she
> thought it was a lake of water and she bared both her calves to
> enter. Solomon told) "This is a palace with crystal floor."
>
> (27:44)[7]

The conclusion and opening of Surah Al-Kahf are identical in terms of asserting that Allah's knowledge is far superior to that of man and that the universe is vaster than what man thinks. Allah's are above and beyond man's access in their broad sense.[8] Were all the trees to turn into pens and all oceans into ink, one cannot inscribe His words[9]:

> (O Prophet), say: "If the sea were to become ink, the record
> of the words of my Lord, the sea would be all used up before
> the words of my Lord exhaust, even if another sea is added as
> ink."
>
> (18: 109)

Elsewhere, the Qur'an states:

---

[7] Surah Al-Naml 27: 44 (This story appears at length in Surah Al-Naml).

[8] In his *Ruh al-Ma'āni*, 'Allamah Alusi maintains: "Words stand for Allah's knowledge and wisdom, power wonders and mysteries. When He intends to declare these, He only says: "Be" and these come into being."

[9] Modern knowledge has spelled out the vastness of this universe, distance between stars, distance between the earth and stars, how light travels, number of stars in each and every galaxy, working of the solar system, size and weight of the sun, wonderful laws of nature, law of gravitation, and cause and effect chain which permeate this universe and maintain the balance in the vast space and ensure the life of the planet earth. Modern knowledge has unravelled the proportion between land and sea and its advantages. Such knowledge was unthinkable in the past. Moreover, the fields of astronomy, biology, anatomy, zoology, botany and other subjects and disciplines have been advanced beyond imagination. There exists a library on every branch of learning. Furthermore, there are excellent laboratories. Yet all this knowledge pales into insignificance in comparison to what is still unknown. There is simply no comparison between the quantum of the two.

If all the trees on earth become pens and the oceans ink, with seven more oceans to supply further ink, the words of Allah will not be exhausted. Allah is Almighty, the Wisest.

(31: 27)

Need for Prophethood and its distinctions

This gives rise to a question: If this universe is beyond man's access owing to its vastness and if all the pens and ink made of all the trees and oceans are insufficient to record Allah's words in that man's intellect cannot grasp this, what is then the way to gain any understanding of the Lord, His being and attributes, the riddle of this life and the path to salvation and success? We (now well that man's knowledge is too limited. The following Qur'anic verse answers the above question:

Say: "I am only a human being like you. However, this message has come to me) "Your Allah is the One True Allah. He who wants to meet his Lord should do good and not take any partner in worshipping his Lord."

(18: 110)

We learn from the above that the revelation sent down by Allah is the only means for having sound understanding and without being guided by this source man cannot expect any success.

Say: "I am only a human being like you. However, this message has come to me: "Your Allah is the One True Allah."

(18: 110)

Final Word

Allah concludes this Surah on the description of the Hereafter, its importance, its exhortation and the call to make this concern the pivot of our life and of our every action.

This concluding note fits in perfectly with the message and spirit permeating the whole Surah:

> He who wants to meet his Lord should do good and not take any partner in worshipping his Lord.
>
> (18: 110)

www.ingramcontent.com/pod-product-compliance
Lightning Source LLC
La Vergne TN
LVHW022054190726
843495LV00014B/1775